people
in the NEWS

Blake Shelton

by Adam Woog

LUCENT BOOKS

A part of Gale, Cengage Learning

GALE
CENGAGE Learning·

Farmington Hills, Mich • San Francisco • New York • Waterville, Maine
Meriden, Conn • Mason, Ohio • Chicago

LIBRARY OF CONGRESS CATALOGING-IN-PUBLICATION DATA

Woog, Adam, 1953-
  Blake Shelton / by Adam Woog.
    pages cm.—(People in the news)
  Includes bibliographical references and index.
  ISBN 978-1-4205-1225-0
  1. Shelton, Blake—Juvenile literature. 2. Country musicians—
Biography—Juvenile literature. I. Title.
  ML3930.S485W66 2015
  782.421642092—dc23
  [B]
                                        2014039617

Lucent Books
27500 Drake Rd.
Farmington Hills, MI 48331

ISBN-13: 978-1-4205-1225-0
ISBN-10: 1-4205-1225-0

Thanks to Misha Berson for her help and expertise.

Printed in the United States of America
2 3 4 5 6 7 19 18 17 16 15

Contents

TN
B
SHE

R

Fame and celebrity are alluring. People are drawn to those who walk in fame's spotlight, whether they are known for great accomplishments or for notorious deeds. The lives of the famous pique public interest and attract attention, perhaps because their experiences seem in some ways so different from, yet in other ways so similar to, our own.

Newspapers, magazines, and television regularly capitalize on this fascination with celebrity by running profiles of famous people. For example, television programs such as *Entertainment Tonight* devote all their programming to stories about entertainment and entertainers. Magazines such as *People* fill their pages with stories of the private lives of famous people. Even newspapers, newsmagazines, and television news frequently delve into the lives of well-known personalities. Despite the number of articles and programs, few provide more than a superficial glimpse at their subjects.

Lucent's People in the News series offers young readers a deeper look into the lives of today's newsmakers, the influences that have shaped them, and the impact they have had in their fields of endeavor and on other people's lives. The subjects of the series hail from many disciplines and walks of life. They include authors, musicians, athletes, political leaders, entertainers, entrepreneurs, and others who have made a mark on modern life and who, in many cases, will continue to do so for years to come.

These biographies are more than factual chronicles. Each book emphasizes the contributions, accomplishments, or deeds that have brought fame or notoriety to the individual and shows how that person has influenced modern life. Authors portray their subjects in a realistic, unsentimental light. For example, Bill Gates—cofounder of the software giant Microsoft—has been instrumental in making personal computers the most vital tool of the modern age. Few dispute his business savvy, his perseverance, or his technical expertise, yet critics say he is ruthless in his dealings with competitors and driven more by his desire to maintain Microsoft's dominance in the computer industry than by an interest in furthering technology.

In these books, young readers will encounter inspiring stories about real people who achieved success despite enormous obstacles. Oprah Winfrey—one of the most powerful, most watched, and wealthiest women in television history—spent the first six years of her life in the care of her grandparents while her unwed mother sought work and a better life elsewhere. Her adolescence was colored by pregnancy at age fourteen, rape, and sexual abuse.

Each author documents and supports his or her work with an array of primary and secondary source quotations taken from diaries, letters, speeches, and interviews. All quotes are footnoted to show readers exactly how and where biographers derive their information and provide guidance for further research. The quotations enliven the text by giving readers eyewitness views of the life and accomplishments of each person covered in the People in the News series.

In addition, each book in the series includes photographs, annotated bibliographies, timelines, and comprehensive indexes. For both the casual reader and the student researcher, the People in the News series offers insight into the lives of today's newsmakers—people who shape the way we live, work, and play in the modern age.

Meet Blake Shelton

A number of years ago, a reporter asked the country music star Blake Shelton what reality show he would like to appear on. The singer was not a fan of reality programming at the time, and he was not enthusiastic about the idea. Referring to a program about hunters, Shelton replied, "I hate reality shows. But if I had to be on one, I'd have to say *Realtree Road Trips* on the Outdoor Channel."[1]

In time the singer changed his tune, and in 2007 he did appear on a couple of reality shows—although they were very different from *Realtree Road Trips*. Both were singing competitions geared toward country fans. He was a judge on the fifth season of *Nashville Star* and on the only season of *Clash of the Choirs*, a miniseries that pit choirs against each other in a competition to raise money for charity.

It seemed that the TV camera "loved" Shelton. His blend of folksy humor, unpretentious charm, and good looks was popular with both shows' viewing audiences—and with television executives as well. In particular, the singer caught the eye of producers who were planning a new singing competition series for NBC, called *The Voice*.

As its millions of fans know well, *The Voice* was—and still is—a smash hit, starting with its first season in 2011. In no small part, this success has been due to a charismatic country singer who did not particularly want to be on reality TV.

A New Plateau

For years before *The Voice* debuted, Blake Shelton had been a star in the world of country. He was well known as a charming, crowd-pleasing performer with an appealing voice, a reputation for hard work, and a knack for choosing good songs. His albums were routinely hitting the top spots on sales charts, and he had already been honored with many music-related awards.

The NBC singing-competition reality series **The Voice** *made Blake Shelton a household name.*

It was not until *The Voice* came along, however, that Shelton skyrocketed to a whole new level of stardom. The show exposed him to a widespread audience, one that might not otherwise listen to country music. The result—for both the singer and country music in general—has been massive popularity.

Shelton has often talked about what a gift this experience has been, and about his gratitude for it. The singer told a reporter, "[I had] always had just enough success to buy me some more tour dates and another record. I was always this close to going to the next level, and I owe [my greater success] to the show for sure."[2]

Besides *The Voice,* another factor in Shelton's life that helped launch him into the world of celebrity was his 2011 marriage to fellow country singer Miranda Lambert. Like Shelton, Lambert already had a flourishing career in music before the two met and fell in love. As a team, however, they ascended to being the number-one power couple in the country music world. Today, they are one of the richest, as well—along with being a top celebrity couple in entertainment overall.

Inevitably, this fame has made them the target of lurid gossip and simply untrue media stories. Shelton and Lambert make fun of these tales—if they pay attention to them at all—but the seemingly nonstop rumors are nonetheless proof of the public's ongoing fascination with the couple.

The Numbers

Gossip and TV aside, perhaps the most important measure of Shelton's success has been his remarkable string of hit albums and singles. The numbers tell the story:

As of mid-2014, Shelton had racked up seventeen songs that hit number one on the country music sales charts—and twelve of them were consecutive. This set a record no country artist has yet broken.

There have been plenty of honors and awards to go with commercial success. These include twenty nominations and eight wins from the Country Music Association (CMA), in categories such as Male Vocalist of the Year, Album of the Year, and Entertainer of the Year. Shelton also won the CMA Entertainer of the Year award for the fourth consecutive time in 2014.

Then there are the fourteen nominations and three wins from another organization, the Academy of Country Music (ACM). There are the seven nominations at the Grammy Awards, the five wins (and many more nominations) at the Country Music Television (CMT) awards ceremony, and the five nominations for the *Billboard* Music Awards. In addition, Shelton has won seven People's Choice Awards, and a nomination and a win at the American Music Awards.

Upon learning that he is to be inducted as a member of the Grand Ole Opry, Blake Shelton hugs his friend and fellow recording artist, Trace Adkins (in hat), during a show at the Opry in September 2010.

Along with all of these awards, Shelton has also earned one of the most prestigious prizes a country performer can earn: membership in the Grand Ole Opry. The Opry is a legendary radio show that has been broadcasting in Nashville since 1925. In the years since then, it has showcased top country, bluegrass, folk, and gospel performers. It is both a theatrical show and a radio program. More than one hundred musicians have cycled through the Opry as cast members over the years, making regular appearances. Hundreds more have appeared as guest performers.

The Opry is country music's equivalent to a hall of fame, like the Rock and Roll Hall of Fame in Cleveland, Ohio. The decision to add a new cast member is up to the Opry's management. It is not an easy or a quick process, and the decision is made on the basis of talent, album sales, and many other factors. So Shelton's invitation to join as a cast member was the country music world's acknowledgment that he had become a true star.

On top of all of these accolades, Shelton was named *People* magazine's "Sexiest Man Alive" in 2012. And then there are other ways to judge his popularity—for example, the fact that as of mid-2014 he had more than seven million Twitter followers and eight million Facebook followers.

Although Shelton has had a meteoric rise to this level of popularity, the journey that led him there began modestly enough, when he was just a typical kid growing up in rural Oklahoma.

Chapter 1

Blake Grows Up

Life in the gently rolling hills of southeastern Oklahoma, as in other parts of the rural United States, is traditional and relaxed. People tend to be stubbornly independent and politically conservative, but also friendly and inviting. Hunting, fishing, and organized sports—especially football—are popular pastimes. Country music—from that of old-time performers such as the legendary Hank Williams to the music of current hitmakers—is also popular in Oklahoma. As his millions of fans know, that is where Blake Shelton fits in.

The Sheltons

Blake Tollison Shelton was born on June 18, 1976, in Ada, Oklahoma, a small town of about 17,000 people. Ada is the seat of Pontotoc County, the headquarters of the Native American group called the Chickasaw Nation and the home of Oklahoma's East Central University. It is also a center for the farming and ranching communities that surround it.

Blake grew up with two older siblings: his brother Richie, from their mother's earlier marriage, and his sister Endy. Richie liked cars and motorcycles, eventually becoming a Motocross champ, while Endy was interested in studying dance and entering beauty pageants.

Their father, Richard Shelton, was a used-car dealer. Dick, as he was known, was a native of Oklahoma and attended school

A storm passes over Ada, Oklahoma, in 2001. Blake Shelton grew up enjoying the animals and outdoor life in the southern Oklahoma city.

in the small towns of Duncan and Lawton. Blake's father served in the U.S. Army during the Korean War (1950–1953). After his time in the service, he worked as a car salesman and, for a period, owned and operated J.R.'s Cars. Over the years he worked for other car agencies in the Ada area, as well.

Blake's father believed in the benefits of hard work—that it keeps a person healthy, independent, and active. He continued to work long after his son became a celebrity who could have easily supported his parents and the rest of the family. In fact, Dick did not retire until 2010.

Meanwhile, Blake's mother, Dorothy, also worked outside the home: She owned a beauty salon in Ada. The singer recalls that his mother's shop was a big part of his childhood. He liked to hang out there when he was little, teasing and flirting with the customers. He recalls: "That's where I learned to b---s--- with girls."[3]

Like her husband, Blake's mother continued to work long after she could have retired on her famous son's money. She and Dick Shelton eventually divorced, and both later remarried. She is now known as Dorothy Shackleford.

Loving Animals

Growing up, Blake was known for his love of nature—a trait that is still an important part of his life. As soon as he could walk, Blake began spending most of his waking hours outdoors, exploring his family's five-acre (2ha) property. His father recalls, "Blake was busy from daylight till dark. I had to put in a PA system in the house so I could holler at him when it was time to come home."[4]

He was especially fond of animals—watching them, playing with them, and learning about them. Much of his time was spent digging under rocks for bugs or catching turtles and crawdads in the creek that ran through his family's property. Blake also loved to be around bigger animals, such as horses and cows.

Blake's love of the animal kingdom was not confined to the outdoors. Sometimes young Blake would bring home the animals and insects he found outside. Over the years he kept an ever-changing menagerie of pets, including two raccoons. His mother gave him the nickname "Toad" because he used to bring so many frogs home. Blake spent so much time pursuing his interest in animals that his mother thought her son would grow up to be a veterinarian or a forest ranger. She recalls, "He loved all animals: grasshoppers, locusts, lizards, snakes, worms. One time I had a flyswatter and I killed a fly, and he cried."[5]

On the other hand, during this period Blake also learned how to hunt and fish, which are still two much-loved pastimes. He comments, "Hunting and fishing [are] my favorite thing[s] to do besides music. I like to go out and be outdoors. . . . I didn't grow up playing video games. I grew up catching crawdads in the creek, and minnows and lizards and snakes. And still to this day, I like to go out and just be in the woods."[6]

Growing up, Blake Shelton would dance around his room pretending to be Hank Williams Jr.—pictured onstage around 1981.

Blake's Other Love

The outdoors were not Blake's only love during the years he was growing up. He was also passionate about music. Blake's brother, Richie, was a big influence in this regard—the older boy's fondness for country music helped shape his younger brother's taste. Listening to his brother's records, Blake would often pretend he was a singer himself. He later recalled, "He would have [country star] Hank Williams Jr. playing so loud that literally the pictures on the walls would be shaking. As a 6- or 7-year-old kid I already was in there with a spoon acting like I was doing a concert."[7]

Blake's love of music was not limited to singing in his room or using spoon as a microphone. His family recalls that he also loved to sing for friends and family whenever he had the chance. Today Shelton is not sure about the source of this desire to perform in public. He asserts, "I don't even know where that came from. I mean, it wasn't like we grew up singing in the living room as a family every night or anything."[8]

His fondness for singing extended beyond the home, too. In junior high and high school, Blake was well known for walking into class singing at the top of his lungs. Such behavior helped make him the constant center of attention—something that he has continued to enjoy as an adult.

Blake's passion for being the center of attention often combined with his goofy sense of humor. Richard Truitt, the teenager's shop teacher at Ada High School, remembers him walking into class every day singing "I'll Be Home for Christmas"—even in summer. Mr. Truitt was apparently not too bothered by Blake's antics, however. After Blake made a wooden guitar the size of a Christmas ornament, he did not bother to keep it—but his teacher did, as a memento of his unusual student.

The First Public Appearances

Blake's gift for music was so promising that his mother decided to enter him in a beauty pageant when he was eight because of the talent segment. He was the only boy in the pageant, competing against fifty little girls, and the experience was followed by several others. He remarked later to reporters that being the only boy embarrassed him. He recalled:

> I still don't know why [she entered me], and it's still the worst experience of my life, being in a pageant. That has to have been the first one, and I can't remember because she put me in, like, two or three in a row there. And I remember singing "Cat Scratch Fever" by Ted Nugent, and "Old Time Rock 'n' Roll" by Bob Seger—[they] were probably my two signature songs.[9]

All That Sauce

Blake Shelton has a reputation for having an open, friendly manner and a down-to-earth, simple approach to life. These traits were ingrained in the singer early on by the rural environment of his childhood. Writer Keith Easton comments:

> Maybe it's the sauce in all that Bob's Barbeque he ate while growing up in Ada, Oklahoma; it could be the wisdom of the feed store philosophers, or what was learned at rodeos, fishing holes, deer blinds and beer joints. But whether in isolation or combination, these all played a big role in creating Blake Shelton—the kid, the boy, the man who has won international recognition as a country and western artist.

Source: Keith Eaton. "Blake Shelton: An Oklahoma Original Is Singing His Way Back Home." *Distinctly Oklahoma*, October 4, 2010. http://distinctlyoklahoma.com/cover -story/blake-shelton-an-oklahoma-original-is-singing-his-way-back-home.

His embarrassing experiences in beauty pageants, however, did not stop Blake from pursuing his love of music. By the age of twelve he was an accomplished guitarist, and he wrote his first song when he was fifteen. His performances led to Blake winning recognition beyond his family and friends.

Notably, when he was fifteen Blake was invited to perform as part of a weekly revue at a theater in downtown Ada. The theater was a historic building dating from the 1920s called the McSwain Theatre. (Today it is still a thriving center for live music, plays, and movies. Its regular features include a monthly country music variety show similar to the one in which Blake appeared as a teenager.) Word about Blake's singing began to spread. By high school he had become a regular feature in a number of country music shows all around central Oklahoma, and at sixteen he won the Denbo Diamond Award, Oklahoma's highest honor for a young musician. By then, Blake was seriously planning a career in the music business. He recalls, "By the time I was 15, I knew this was what I wanted to do with my life . . . [I] knew I wanted to be famous, I wanted to be involved in country music."[10]

Pleasing the Audience

These early shows taught the singer about working a stage—that is, creating an exciting performance that engages an audience. He was a natural performer, always at ease in the limelight. His sister, Endy, recalls, "Being in front of an audience never fazed him. The way he is on camera now is exactly the way he was when he was 10 years old."[11]

During this period, however, his stage presence did not exactly signal the stylish image he would project as an adult. Referring to the short-in-front, long-in-back hairstyle (known as the mullet) favored by many boys and men at the time, Endy recalls, "He didn't look quite like he does now. He was a little chubbier, he had a mullet going on, glasses. He didn't have too much success [with looking fashionable]."[12]

Of course, Blake's life did not completely revolve around music and honing his stage presence. He also took part in typical teenage activities, such as dating and hanging out with friends. He was a big kid who was growing fast toward his eventual height of six feet five inches, so naturally he loved to eat, and to eat a lot. He could cook some, too: He once won a chili cook-off as part of a high school "bachelor cooking" class.

On the other hand, during his high school years there were things that did not interest him. For example, despite his rugged build Blake was not very interested in playing organized sports—an unusual thing for a young man in Oklahoma, where sports (especially football) are considered an important part of growing up. The singer later claimed that he was a little afraid of violent-contact sports. He told a reporter, "I'm too big of a [wimp], man."[13]

This tendency to avoid aggressive physical contact extended to other areas of Blake's life, as well. He never got into serious trouble fighting other kids. He also avoided breaking the law during his high school years—Shelton later remarked that he was too afraid of getting caught by his family or the authorities.

Blake's fear of getting in trouble, however, did not curb his goofy sense of humor—especially his love for playing pranks. One time he propped up the carcass of a dead deer on the driver's side of his friend's pickup truck to watch what happened when the friend saw it. (His friend, the singer recalls, was pretty freaked out.) Blake's mischievous sense of humor was apparent to everyone—his fellow students at Ada High School repeatedly voted him class clown.

Tragedy

Overall, Blake's life was happy during these years, but he and his family also experienced a major tragedy. The singer's older brother, Richie, was killed in a car accident when he was only twenty-four years old.

Blake was just fourteen when it happened. He remembers standing outside the family's house, waiting for a friend to pick him up to go to school, when he heard ambulances go by. He recalls, "I didn't think anything of it. When I got to school and Dad pulled me out of class, I thought, 'Oh. . . . That's what I heard.'"[14]

Richie had been driving with his girlfriend when they slammed into the back of a school bus. The girlfriend was driving, Richie was in the passenger seat, and the girlfriend's four-year-old son was in the back. All three of them died.

Not surprisingly, Blake was devastated by his brother's death. He recalls, "The guy was my hero. Talk about worship—[to me] he was the coolest guy on earth."[15]

Richie was buried in McGee Cemetery in the town of Stratford, in neighboring Garvin County. After the funeral, Blake gathered mementos of his beloved brother, in particular, Richie's prized record collection, which helped Blake through his period of grief. The singer later told a reporter, "The family gave me all his albums and things like that. I just listened to them over and over again to feel like he was there."[16]

Many years later, Blake would honor Richie by writing a poignant song in his memory. Before that could happen, however, the budding musician needed to try his hand at making it in a notoriously tough field: the music business.

Next Stop: Nashville

As a young boy, Blake envisioned for himself nothing more ambitious than working in construction. Like many boys at that age, he recalls, "I was always fascinated with backhoes and bulldozers. . . ."[17] By Blake's teen years, however, those modest plans had gone by the wayside. He instead set his sights on a career in country music; nothing else appealed to him. He later told a reporter what would have happened if he had not become a singer:

> I would probably be homeless because I do not know anything else that I would want to do with my life. I don't know. I would probably be in trouble somewhere because it was the only thing that I was interested in, and if I wasn't doing music, I was just goofing off. And there's nothing but trouble that can come from somebody who has no ambition and nothing they want to do with their life.[18]

To pursue his dream, the logical step was clearly a move to Nashville, Tennessee, which for decades had been (and still is) the undisputed center of country music. The vast majority of country-related record companies, clubs, agents, and publishing companies are headquartered in Music City, as it is known.

For an aspiring country singer, there are few other options. Journalist Keith Eaton comments:

> If you want to be in the movies, you hit Sunset and Vine [in Hollywood, California]; aspire to make your fortune in finance, then Wall Street's your Mecca. But if you're serious, talented, brash and long to "kick out the footlights" at every C&W [country and western] venue in the states, then Nashville's Music Row, the confluence of Demonbreun Street, Division Street, 16th Avenue South and

Music Square East and West, is your destination, and likely your home for decades.[19]

Meeting Mae Boren Axton

A move to Nashville was especially smart for someone like Blake, who was drawn to mainstream, traditional country music. This is the type of country that Nashville specializes in, while other parts of the United States are associated with other distinctive (if less popular) country styles. For example, Texas-style music was made famous by such singers as Willie Nelson, Kris Kristof-

Nashville, Tennessee, is widely regarded as the home of country music.

ferson, and Robert Earl Keen. Another example was the "Bakersfield Sound" out of California, which was popularized by artists such as Merle Haggard, Dwight Yoakum, and Brad Paisley.

Blake was more interested in the mainstream than in these various outcroppings of country music. He comments, "It was always Nashville or bust for me. I knew the action and sound of Austin, Bakersfield and L.A., but it wasn't my thing."[20]

Blake received a major boost toward a career in Nashville while he was still attending Ada High School and playing small shows around the region. This was a chance meeting with someone who would prove to change the teenager's life: Mae Boren Axton, a Texas native who had close ties to Blake's hometown of Ada.

Axton was a legendary figure in the world of country music, the writer or co-writer of some two hundred songs. Many of them had become hits, especially "Heartbreak Hotel"—Elvis Presley's first single and the recording that launched his spectacular career. The veteran songwriter was also well known for mentoring a number of talented newcomers. For example, she played key roles in helping the careers of Willie Nelson and Reba McEntire, who, like Blake, is a native of Oklahoma.

Good Advice

Blake met Axton when the young musician performed at a concert honoring her. Blake impressed the veteran songwriter, and she gave him a simple but valuable piece of advice: He really should move to Nashville if he was serious. The singer recalls, "That was all the encouragement I needed. That was the first person I'd ever met that was actually in the [professional] music industry and so it was a real big deal to me just to meet her and to have her tell me that. It made what I was doing seem real for a change."[21]

In truth, the songwriter's advice only confirmed what Blake already knew. Two weeks after his high school graduation, the teenager loaded all of his possessions into the back of a pickup

The skyline of Nashville, Tennessee, is seen from the Cumberland River in 2001. It was the largest city Blake Shelton had ever seen when he moved there in 1993.

and headed east. The aspiring singer later recalled that no one in his family was surprised. He told a reporter, "I think it was just understood that when I graduated, that was my destiny."[22]

Nashville was by far the biggest city that Blake had ever seen, and it was abuzz with energy stemming from the countless musicians—professionals and hopefuls—who were part of the lively scene. When Blake arrived, he felt a little intimidated. He persevered, however, even though he knew it might involve years of scuffling before he found success.

Blake's first task was to find a cheap apartment. He did, but he was so young that some friends of the Shelton family who lived in Nashville had to cosign contracts to ensure that the apartment's gas and electric bills would be paid.

A Succession of Jobs

The aspiring singer's next step was to find work. At first, Blake found only a succession of low-paying odd jobs. One of these, for example, was painting signs. He also did occasional construction work. Blake was no stranger to such outdoor labor: As a high school student, he spent several summers painting and roofing houses with his stepfather, Mike Shackleford.

Blake also worked for a time at a small publishing company, Balmur Music. His job there was to make copies of recordings by other musicians. It was dull, but at least it was connected to the music industry. Problems arose, however, because Blake enjoyed hanging out with the songwriters who came in. He spent too much time talking with them, and it was not long before he was fired for ignoring his duties.

He had several other occupations along the way, only some of them associated with music. The singer later commented, "There's no telling how many jobs I went through—four or five. At that point, I had worked my way into the [music] community enough that I started singing a lot of demos."[23] (A "demo," short for "demonstration," is a rough recording made by songwriters and singers to show off their talents to record companies when seeking a contract.) He also briefly worked as a staff songwriter for Tree, another music publishing company.

All of these were just placeholder jobs, ways to earn money while working toward a bigger goal. Moving to Nashville had been a bold move: Blake had left his familiar home, and his time in Music City had so far been without notable success. But things were about to change.

Chapter 2

Scuffling

During his first few years in Nashville, Shelton's family was naturally worried about him. They wondered if he would get tired of trying to crack the professional music scene and return home. That, of course, was not what happened. His father later joked, "[H]e sure fooled me. He stuck it out."[24]

Like any stubborn teenager, Shelton resisted following his family's advice. Just a few weeks after the aspiring singer arrived in Nashville, Dick Shelton sent him a letter with advice on living on his own. Shelton recalls:

> It was, like, five pages thick. The first couple lines said, "Hey, I didn't get a chance to tell you some things that I wanted to tell you about entering the world," and as soon as I read that, I folded it back up. I didn't want to hear it. I was 17. I didn't want to be told what to do.[25]

Perseverance

Shelton may have ignored his father's advice, but he did accept the help and encouragement of another person: Mae Boren Axton. She found him one of his first jobs—he spent two weeks painting her house. Axton took him under her wing in other ways and even held a party, complete with cake, to celebrate Shelton's eighteenth birthday—his first one away from home. The young man eventually grew so close to the songwriter that he sometimes called her Mama Mae.

Singer-songwriter and actor Hoyt Axton gave a young Blake Shelton advice about the music industry. Axton's mother, legendary songwriter Mae Boren Axton, was also instrumental in shaping Shelton's career.

Axton was more than a close friend and a surrogate family member. She also introduced Shelton to a number of people in the music industry—a crucial step in advancing his career. Not only was her advice to him good, it was also freely given. Blake later recalled, "It was like my security blanket. I always knew if I needed something or if I had a question, I could call Mae. If she didn't know, she would know by the end of the day."[26]

Shelton also received encouragement from another Axton: Mae's son Hoyt, who was already well established as a singer, songwriter, and occasional actor. When he was not on the road, Hoyt Axton often parked his band's tour bus in his mother's driveway. Shelton spent hours in the bus with Hoyt, playing and talking about music.

This period of Shelton's life was hard—he had so far achieved virtually no success toward his goal. Nonetheless, the singer kept at it. Today, he recommends the same course of action for anyone else interested in a career like his. He told a reporter:

> The only real good advice I have is to move to Nashville and be prepared to be told "no" so many times that it makes you sick. Because that's what is going to happen when you get there. People are gonna tell you you're not good enough, or they're not even gonna talk to you, period. It takes time and it takes patience, but the one thing I do know about this business is that it is not always based on talent. It is based on timing and luck and who you know.[27]

Meeting Bobby Braddock

While his various day jobs paid the bills, Shelton was at the same time working hard on his songwriting and singing. He was also living hard, drinking, and partying until the wee hours of the morning. Shelton has compared his lifestyle as a young man to the lyrics of a typical country song: "I would wake up in the morning, hung over from the night before, especially at that age. I'd try to write a song . . . and do it all over again that night."[28]

Shelton also sang in public wherever he could, notably at the open-mike nights that many clubs around Nashville regularly held (and still do). He was a popular artist on this modest circuit, where unpaid singers appear in front of small audiences to hone their skills. Meanwhile, as a songwriter, Shelton began to attract attention from some of Nashville's major music publishers, including Warner/Chappell Music and Jerry Crutchfield Music. They were able to convince established performers to record a few of his songs.

Genuine success eluded the musician, however, until he connected with another figure who, like Mae Boren Axton, would change his life. This was a well-known songwriter named Bobby Braddock.

Since the 1970s, Braddock had been a respected and successful figure on the Nashville music scene. By the time he and Shelton connected, Braddock already had more than thirty top-ten hits to his credit. Notably, he wrote or co-wrote such now-classic hits as "D-I-V-O-R-C-E," a number-one hit by Tammy Wynette in 1968, and "He Stopped Loving Her Today," which was first recorded by George Jones in 1980. (That song continues to be a success and has been covered by many artists since then. According to *Allmusic* magazine, in the 1990s a survey of fans and industry insiders voted "He Stopped Loving Her Today" as the best country song ever written.)

During this period, Braddock was expanding his career by becoming a producer—that is, a professional who creates and oversees recordings for singers—rather than just writing the songs. A friend and fellow songwriter, Michael Kosser, began enthusiastically telling Braddock about an unknown singer he had heard. One day Kosser called Braddock to play him a demo over the phone. Braddock later recalled, "I said, 'The song's okay,

Songwriter and producer Bobby Braddock is photographed in Nashville in 2011, shortly before being inducted into the Country Music Hall of Fame. Braddock was instrumental in getting Blake Shelton his first record deal.

but who's that guy singing?' He said, 'That's the kid I was telling you about.'"[29]

The "kid," of course, was Blake Shelton. Soon Braddock arranged to meet the singer in person. The two got along well, liked and respected each other's work, and agreed to team up. Braddock recalls, "I thought he had what it took to be a superstar. One thing he has, and it comes through when he's singing live or in the studio, is a certain electricity and charisma. Not a lot of people have it."[30]

Giant Records

The first order of business for Shelton and Braddock was to cut demos, the rough versions of songs that songwriters and singers use to show off their strengths. The compositions they chose were a mix of songs written by Shelton alone, Shelton and Braddock together, and others. Braddock took copies of these recordings around town, trying to interest a record label in signing the performer. He had little success at first.

Despite Braddock's impressive track record and his prominence in the Nashville music community, no record company executives were willing to take a chance on an unknown singer. Braddock and Shelton tried almost every place in town before they hit pay dirt. They found a label called Giant Records that was interested in them.

A major reason for this interest was that the executives at Giant liked one particular song Braddock had written: "Same Old Song." It is a satirical tune that makes fun of the bland, stereotyped, commercial nature of so much modern country music. The song laments the genre's lack of powerful emotion and original style.

The song was a good one, thoughtful and funny and catchy, and the record company executives saw it as a potential hit. Braddock held out, though, for something more than merely selling the rights to record one song. He told the people at Giant that they could have the tune only if Shelton sang it and signed a contract for an album. The strategy worked, as Shelton recalls: "That kinda helped push it over the edge."[31]

An Early Role Model

Every performer has favorite established artists who serve as role models. In Shelton's case, one of his most important role models early in his career was the singer Trace Adkins, who later became a close friend and occasional collaborator. Shelton comments:

> I first moved to Nashville in 1994, and once you work your way into the community, you find out what's going on with the record industry. I remember Trace Adkins was the first name that I ever heard that was, like, "Hey, this guy just got a record deal." I followed him very closely through the years before I ever got my opportunity to make a record. I felt like I had a lot invested in his career emotionally, just watching him. Obviously, I was a fan of his music. I mean he's a true country artist.
>
> Once I got my opportunity to start having songs out on the radio and things like that in 2001, Trace was one of the guys I was excited to finally meet. I sound like a freak fan or something, but he was everything that I had imagined him to be—his personality, his sense of humor, everything about him. He's just that guy. . . . He's always been one of my favorite artists and someone I've looked up to as a person. There's nothing about him that I don't think is cool. I would never say this stuff to his face, but I just think he's a bad-ass guy.

Source: Craig Shelburne. "Blake Shelton Digs Up the Dirt on *Hillbilly Bone.*" *CMT Insider News Now,* March 19, 2010. www .cmt.com/news/country-music/1634321 /blake-shelton-digs-up-the-dirt-on-hill billy-bone-part-1-of-2.jhtml.

Trace Adkins and Blake Shelton attend the 2009 Academy of Country Music Awards in Las Vegas, Nevada.

Finding "Austin"

In 1998 Shelton and Braddock reached an agreement with Giant, despite rumors about the company that were spreading on Nashville's grapevine. According to these rumors, Giant was in serious financial trouble and was in danger of closing down.

As a result, the deal had both good and bad elements. On the one hand, Shelton was naturally thrilled to have a record contract, but on the other hand, he was worried that Giant's financial problems might lead to trouble later on. He recalls, "From the day I signed with that record company, I was excited and had a sick feeling at the same time."[32]

Shelton formally signed his contract with Giant Records in July 1998 and soon went into the studio to cut his first album. He and Braddock drew up a list of songs they wanted to include. One of them, "Austin," was a new tune written by an unknown pair, David Kent and Kirsti Manna. It is a sweet, poignant story about a woman living in Austin, Texas, who is trying to reconnect with a former lover (or husband—the song does not specify which). When she left, she did not leave a number where he could reach her. Almost a year later, however, she realizes that she misses him terribly and works up the courage to call him.

The man is not at home, so she hears a message on his voicemail. To her shocked surprise, it ends with a reference to her: "And P.S.—If this is Austin, I still love you."[33] She is taken aback and hangs up, too scared to leave a message. She eventually does call back three days later, this time leaving her phone number. When he returns the call, he hears her voice; thinking at first that he has gotten a recording, he hears her confess that she still loves him. However, it is not a recording—she has answered the phone in person, and she confesses that she still deeply loves him.

Shelton was immediately drawn to "Austin." He later told a reporter, "I loved the song but I didn't know if it would work for me, if I could sell it." Nonetheless, he went home and learned it on his guitar, growing more assured. "That night, I knew it was going to work for me and I was getting excited."[34]

One reason he fell in love with the song was that it seemed true to life—including his own. He could identify strongly with the story's message. He told a reporter, "I've had girlfriends I've gotten back together with after we'd broken up, and it never worked out. But 'Austin' relates to all of those situations, whether it [the situation] works out or not. It's really about second chances."[35]

Beginning with this period in his life, much of the singer's success can be attributed to his ability to choose excellent material like "Austin," regardless of who wrote the song. He is quick to acknowledge that, in his opinion, choosing good material may be the most important part of a singer's success. Shelton comments, "That's the hardest thing about making a record—finding those songs that you instantly love that you don't instantly get tired of."[36]

Taking a Chance

The story behind how the song came to Shelton's attention is also about taking risks and getting second chances. Its writers, Kirsti Manna and David Kent, had already offered it to several record companies around Nashville. The songwriters were unknown, however, so it was unlikely that one of their compositions would be seriously considered right away.

Then an executive at Giant Records named Debbie Zavitson took a chance. She was in the habit of listening to any demo that came her way—even from unknown singers and composers. When she heard the song she loved it, and she made sure that Shelton heard it, too. In the years after recording "Austin," the singer has often told reporters that he will always be grateful to Zavitson for keeping her ears open and being persistent in following her instincts. He says about her:

> She'd give something a chance, at least for a few seconds. . . . It never stops. Every day, somebody has a song they want you to hear, and you're stupid if you don't listen to it because you never know what you may find. "Austin" was one of those songs that nobody would give a chance

Blake Shelton poses in a publicity photo in 1998, when he was promoting his hit debut single, "Austin."

because it didn't come from well-known writers or well-known publishers. Luckily for me, I wasn't a well-known artist at the time. So you just never know.[37]

Once Shelton had practiced the song enough and become comfortable with it, he was eager to record it. There was almost nothing that needed to be done to the composition before that could take place—except for one thing. Bobby Braddock felt that its original title, "If This Is Austin," was too long. He suggested that it be shortened. David Kent, one of the songwriters, recalls, "Bobby said he could just see it as one word, 'Austin,' sitting up there at the top of the charts. We said, 'Hey, Blake's singing the daylights out of it—you can call it 'Boston' if you like!'"[38]

The First Single

The process of recording "Austin" and the album's other songs, and then releasing them to the public, was relatively slow. Three years passed between the day the singer signed with Giant and the appearance in 2001 of his self-titled debut, *Blake Shelton*.

This debut album was a mix of songs, but they reflected a general attitude that has held all through Shelton's career. He has sought to avoid dull compositions that simply revisit the themes of Nashville commercial music. This reflects his different outlook on the country music industry—one that he shared with Braddock.

The Braddock-penned "Same Old Song" on that first album is a good example of this. It takes aim at the light, happy lyrics that have come to dominate the country charts. In this case, his record company did not challenge Shelton's take on the sweet-as-syrup country business. Shelton insisted that the other songs on the album also avoid common country music clichés. He later told a reporter, "I think my music is pretty much G-rated compared to a lot of the stuff you hear, so I really don't think that I'm pushing the envelope. I just don't want to be vanilla, and I think [fans] understand it."[39]

As is often true in the music business, the first single from the recording was released shortly before the full album. The record company chose "Austin" for this honor. The original plan had been to release another song, this one written by Braddock—"I Wanna Talk About Me"—as the first single. Eventually the executives at Giant decided against including that song on the album altogether. (Another performer, Toby Keith, later recorded "I Wanna Talk About Me" and took it to number one on the sales charts.)

Almost immediately after the single of "Austin" was released, Shelton encountered a serious problem. This obstacle had the potential to wreck his career (or at least significantly slow him down) right when he was getting started. Just a few weeks after the release of "Austin," the rumors about Giant proved to be true—the company folded. Shelton suddenly found himself under contract to a record company that was no longer putting out records.

Saving "Austin"

Fortunately for Shelton, an executive at Giant, Fritz Kuhlman, was aware that the company was about to close its doors.

Blake Shelton poses with John Esposito, the president of Warner Bros. Nashville, at a 2011 event. The record company released Shelton's first single and album after his original record company went out of business.

Kuhlman liked Shelton's song and, before the end came, secretly arranged for it to go public. He made a hundred copies of the single and sent them to radio stations around the country, several weeks before its official release date. It was an excellent move—radio stations liked the song and began playing it often. Shelton later commented that hearing himself on the radio was a strange experience. He told a reporter at the time, "It almost feels like I'm doing the impossible. I didn't think I'd become [like] somebody that I idolized when I was 15. . . . I've done the thing that only a handful of people get to do. I'm hearing my songs on the radio. It really freaks me out."[40]

A Hit

The listening public liked the single, and it was an immediate hit. Right away, "Austin" charted—that is, it appeared on the Hot Country Songs sales chart of *Billboard*, the music industry's major magazine. Its success led to an increasing number of opportunities for Shelton to perform in concert. The song continued to climb the charts, eventually spending five weeks as the number-one country song in the nation.

Shelton, surprised at the sudden positive response, gave all the credit to the song—not his performance of it. He commented at the time, "I hate to think now about coming out with a different song. I can't think of a better situation to have, for your first single to be doing this."[41]

Luckily for him, Giant was able to meet the sudden demand for the song even after the company officially closed. This was because Giant was owned by Warner Bros., one of the world's biggest record companies, and Warner was able to keep manufacturing recordings that would have previously been released on the Giant label.

The Impact a Song Can Have

Since its release, the tenderness of "Austin" has touched many people over the years with its message: that love can have a

Not Vanilla

Shelton has always been more interested in singing mainstream country music, as opposed to the distinctive and less commercial styles developed in places like California and Texas. However, he is also critical of the blandness of so many commercial Nashville country songs. A good example of this is "Same Old Song," from his debut album. Written by his early mentor and producer, Bobby Braddock, it mocks compositions that rely on light, happy lyrics—that is, the kind of songs that currently dominate the country charts. Shelton has this to say about it:

> Everything [on the album] had to live up to that song or it wouldn't make it onto the album [because] I'd be contradicting myself. . . . I want to be politically incorrect because that's life, that's reality.
>
> I think my music is pretty much G-rated compared to a lot of the stuff you hear, so I really don't think that I'm pushing the envelope. I just don't want to be vanilla, and I think they understand it. Like with [the song] "Ol' Red," in the first couple lines of the song, the guy kills somebody. Well, 15 years ago nobody would blink twice at that. Now, all of a sudden, that's an issue. And it's just a story.

Source: "Hotstar: Blake Shelton." *Pollstar*, December 7, 2001. www.pollstar.com /hotstar_article.aspx?ID=75738.

second chance to ignite after it has seemingly failed. The song's co-composer, David Kent, comments:

> We've gotten so much e-mail from people whose lives have been changed. One lady said she'd left her husband after 15 years, thinking she wasn't happy, and didn't tell him where she was going. She'd been away a year, not knowing what to do—then she heard "Austin."

She called her husband and left her number on his machine, he called her back that night, and now they're working on their relationship. Now, there's the real reason you write a song.[42]

Not surprisingly, the success of the single spurred the sales of the full album, *Blake Shelton*. Overall, critics liked the album as much as the public did. One reviewer, writer Maria Konicki Dinoia, commented, "This . . . is an earnest debut full of lots of promise and originality. [It is] an album destined for musical greatness."[43]

Not every reviewer was as enthusiastic, however. Scott Homewood, writing in *Country Standard Time*, commented, "[H]is songs strain to sound more important and weighty than they really are. . . . While his voice sounds warm and radio-friendly, this album just smacks of being assembled with the intent on capturing the burgeoning alternative country market."[44]

The Hair Issue

During these early years of his career, Shelton continued to hone his singing, songwriting, and onstage performances. In the opinion of some, though, one aspect of his public appearance still needed work: his fashion sense. Shelton was still far from looking like the stylish celebrity he is today.

In particular, there was the hair issue. Especially once his fame was established, Shelton's hair was a major topic for intense discussions by reporters and fans. It remained the same unstylish mullet that he had worn in his teenage years. Shelton says he kept it that way mainly because he liked it—but also simply because he wanted to annoy other people. During this period he commented:

I choose to keep my hair long because it has been long since I was 12 years old. It doesn't matter to me what other people do with their hair, and I do not think they are interested in how I wear my hair. Basically, it has gotten to the point where it is just a matter of pride.

Blake Shelton shows off his long curls in a publicity photo in 2001.

And I know it looks like crap, but it is just more fun to me to irritate people than cut my hair to satisfy them. . . . And my answer [for people who criticize] is that you ought to call Willie Nelson up and tell him that it is not cool to have long hair.[45]

Today Shelton's mullet and chubby looks are long gone, jettisoned in favor of a sophisticated, short-haired look. The singer is also particular about other aspects of personal style. He once told a reporter that he finds it unacceptable when he sees "somebody standing on the stage . . . or some formal place and they're wearing a T-shirt and baseball cap." He also hates bare feet, pleading with other artists to "cover [their] stinkin', nasty feet" in music videos. . . . Flip-flops aren't even acceptable."[46]

Shelton's early years in Nashville had been a long and hard struggle. The singer had paid his dues, as performers often say about their years of scuffling for a living. After he made the connection with Braddock, however, things began to move more quickly, and now Shelton was about to move to a new level of success.

Chapter 3

Breakthrough

The sales of Shelton's music showed that the public clearly liked his music, and after the success of "Austin," the executives at Warner Records agreed. The company had the option to pick up the contracts of Giant's artists, and its executives chose to absorb Shelton into their organization. He now had a powerhouse company behind him to promote and distribute his records.

There were other promising signs as well. Notably, the Academy of Country Music gave him a prestigious honor: It nominated him for their "Top New Male Vocalist" award based on the strength of the singer's debut album. He was nominated the following year, 2002, as well. He did not win either time, but just being nominated was an honor and gave a major boost to his career.

Still, despite his growing recognition and impressive sales figures, Shelton did not immediately become a major star. Having a successful first single and album, he discovered, was not enough to guarantee long-lasting success. The second single pulled from the album ("All Over Me") did not do as well as hoped on the sales charts. Needless to say, this was a serious disappointment. The singer recalls, "I was like . . . this is easy! And then the next single came out, and it died a horrible death."[47]

Despite the unsatisfactory sales of "All Over Me," however, Shelton's years of scuffling were over. He was finally able to quit his sporadic day jobs. For the first time in his life, he was able to work steadily and full-time as a musician and songwriter.

Blake Shelton participates in the Academy of Country Music's Bill Boyd Celebrity Golf Classic in 2001, his first year as an ACM nominee.

Not surprisingly, Shelton was delighted. He acknowledged that all the credit should go to "Austin." As he told a reporter at the time, "It was just one of those songs that couldn't be stopped. I was just the lucky guy who got my hands on it. I think the power of that song is what brought me through that transition [to a successful career. The audience attends concerts] because of that song and it has nothing to do with me. I've got a ways to go before people will show up just because they see my name there."[48]

The Dreamer

After hitting it big with his first release, Shelton now faced the challenge of maintaining the momentum, continuing to write and perform songs that he hoped would be solid hits. He continued to tour and play in concert—for bigger venues now,

Miranda Turns Pro

Blake and his future wife had early careers that in some ways were similar. For one thing, both were playing professionally early on.

By seventeen Miranda had a regular weekend engagement at a dance hall in Longview, near her East Texas home. Over the next few years her reputation grew and she began steadily touring with her backing musicians, the Texas Pride Band, at first regionally and then around the country.

She usually traveled on a bus with a dozen musicians and roadies—all of them male. Not surprisingly, it was a demanding life. At one point, Lambert called her business manager and said, "I need you to check: How much is it to live in an insane asylum and how much is it for a second bus? Because I either have to do one or the other."

But after years of scuffling, the aspiring singer received a major break: an appearance in 2003, when she was twenty, on a reality talent show called *Nashville Star*. Miranda came in third and was given a recording contract with a major label. That turned out pretty well: Her first album, *Kerosene*, was released in 2005 and became a smash: It produced four Top 40 hits and went platinum, meaning it sold one million copies.

Source: Meryl Gordon. "Miranda Lambert: Nashville's Shooting Star." *Ladies Home Journal*, March 2011. www.lhj.com/style/covers/miranda-lambert.

rather than open-mike nights for amateurs—and he also released a second album, 2002's *The Dreamer*.

As with his first recordings, both the album and its first single rocketed up the charts. In particular, *The Dreamer*'s first single, "The Baby," reached number one on the *Billboard* chart and stayed there for three weeks.

This poignant song is told from the point of view of the youngest child in a family. Since he was the youngest, his mother indulged him and tended to forgive him when he did something bad—and suggested that, even after he grew up, he was still her "baby." The song goes on to describe the singer's feelings when his mother is dying and he is far away. He rushes to be with her, but he arrives too late to say goodbye. The song's final lines go on to describe how the singer kisses his dead mother and then goes on to cry like a baby.

Roots in Real Life

The song has its roots in real life: It was based on the relationship that one of its writers, Michael White, had with his mother. White told a reporter, "[T]he one thing that it teaches me, and hopefully everyone who hears the song, is not to take your family for granted, and try to at least stay in touch with them."[49] Shelton adds his own take on the song's tenderness: "I feel a responsibility when I sing that song, or any song, to deliver it in a way that's believable and emotional to people."[50]

Following the pattern of the singles taken from his debut album, *The Dreamer's* second and third singles ("Heavy Liftin'" and "Playboys of the Southwestern World") made the best-seller charts but failed to reach the top slot. The album itself, meanwhile, went gold, which is the music industry's term for records that hit figures of 500,000 copies sold and $1,000,000 in sales.

Shelton's career, however, was not always a steady uphill climb during this period. There were many ups and downs. He told a reporter in 2003:

> We were laughing with my record company the other day, every time we think we've got my career under control, and got a good handle on it, there's another hurdle. It's either looking for a tour to get on, or a single doesn't do as well as you think it will, or album sales aren't as good as you thought they would be. And then on the other hand, a single will be No. 1 on the pop charts.[51]

Marrying Kaynette

In 2003 the singer received another honor from the Academy of Country Music: along with Tracy Byrd, Andy Griggs, and Mont-

Hard Lessons for a Future Songwriter

Miranda Lambert's early life was light-years away from the typically all-American childhood her future husband had. She was born in 1983 and grew up in the East Texas town of Lindale as part of a solidly middle-class family.

But when Texas's booming oil economy crashed later in the 1980s, countless businesses and families fell into chaos. Among the casualties was her parents' private investigation firm. Lambert recalls, "I was in first grade and we lost everything. I remember every detail about it, every tear."

At their lowest point the Lamberts lost their home and had to move into a shabby rental house. They survived on food they grew and livestock they kept, supplemented by meat her father brought back from hunting trips.

Financial hardships taught young Miranda some hard lessons. So did what she saw through her mother's church-related involvement with a shelter for abused women. But Miranda's experiences also had a silver lining: They provided the inspiration for much of her music. Only half-joking, she has commented that bad times are good for creative artists:

> Being happy is horrible for songwriting, especially for country music. We just want to write about leaving and sadness. We're all better when we're tormented. I have to put myself in a dark place if I want to write something good.

Source: Meryl Gordon. "Miranda Lambert: Nashville's Shooting Star." *Ladies Home Journal*, March 2011. www.lhj.com/style/covers/miranda-lambert.

gomery Gentry, the organization nominated him in the "Vocal Event of the Year" award (a specific category for songs featuring multiple headliners) for his participation in "The Truth About Men," the title song of Byrd's 2003 album.

The biggest event in Shelton's life, however, was not vocal: The singer married his longtime girlfriend, a schoolteacher named Kaynette Gern. They had met in Ada, Oklahoma, just after she finished high school and had been a couple for five years.

Blake Shelton and his wife, Kaynette Gern, arrive at the 2005 CMT Music Awards in Nashville, Tennessee. The couple divorced the next year.

The ceremony was small, attended only by a few friends and family. The two wanted it that way. Shelton stated at the time, "Our whole lives are always in the public eye, plus we live on a bus with 10 other people. There's just always people around. We never have time for us, so it seemed like the perfect way to do this. It was a moment we would always share, knowing it was just the two of us."[52]

Shelton sang at the wedding—which took place while he was in the middle of a tour with fellow singer Toby Keith—but the priest who officiated did not realize who Shelton was. The singer recalls, "We were cracking up because after the ceremony the preacher said, 'You know, we've had some people sing songs. You did better than a lot of people. You were actually on key a little bit, so that was nice for a change.' We thought that was really funny!"[53]

Kat, as his new wife was called, acted for a time as his road manager, but this arrangement, and the marriage itself, proved to have troubles. Shelton later said that he was simply not ready to be a husband. He and Kat were divorced in 2006; she later moved to Kansas, remarried, and found work as a math teacher.

Maintaining the Momentum

Throughout this period, Shelton continued to work hard at boosting the upward trend of his career. This required crisscrossing the country on a tour bus with his backing musicians to make some 120 performances a year, often as the opening act for a bigger star.

Maintaining this grueling tour schedule was exhausting. His simple life in Oklahoma was a distant memory, but the singer continued to bear in mind that he had to give it his all every night. Shelton understood that his fans were the reason for his success, and he has always tried to return the favor by delivering a good show. He comments, "I am going to give them every ounce of me on that stage because they deserve it."[54]

While on tour, Shelton developed a number of pre-show rituals—that is, things he always did before going on stage. For example, he always stuck chewing gum on the back of the neck

Blake Shelton performs at a venue near Atlanta, Georgia, in 2006, a period of his career when he played up to 120 concerts a year.

of his guitar. He told a reporter, "If you ever come to one of my shows and if I turn around, you can look on the back of my guitar and I promise you, you will see a big wad of gum there."[55] Shelton persevered in the studio as well, releasing a third album in 2004. *Blake Shelton's Barn and Grill* had mixed but overall good sales after its release in 2004. Its first single, "When Somebody Knows You That Well," never went higher than thirty-seven on the sales chart, but—in a reversal from the earlier pattern—the next singles drawn from the album did better.

Notably, there was the cleverly titled "Some Beach"—which may sound like a word with a saltier meaning when pronounced with a Southern accent—a song about the frustrations of daily life and what the singer does to overcome them. Whenever he is stuck in traffic or is otherwise irritated, he dreams about "some beach" where life is idyllic. The song was a hit, reaching number one on the *Billboard* chart and staying there for four weeks.

Meeting Miranda

By the mid-2000s, things were still moving fast for Shelton. He was steadily recording and had begun to headline shows nationally, and each release was routinely hitting the tops of the sales charts. Not surprisingly, he was happy and grateful with his progress, but he was not the only person in Nashville who was delighted. Debbie Zavitson, the record company executive who had first spotted a potential hit in "Austin," commented:

Blake Shelton and Miranda Lambert hug during a performance at an ACM awards event in 2009. The couple met while performing on a CMT show a few years earlier.

[Blake's] voice is just so sincere when you hear him sing, and his songs are the same way. And he's just an honorable, very gracious man. I can't tell you enough how his sense of honor and loyalty is missing in people today. Here in Nashville, everybody's pulling for Blake because he's so well liked, and when somebody like him is such a generally nice guy [and] has success, it's like, "Yay, happy ending."[56]

The steady rise of Shelton's career was by no means the only major event in his life during this period. Notably, in 2005 he shared a stage for the first time with a Texas-born singer named Miranda Lambert.

The two first met when they were paired on a televised Nashville show, performing a song called "You're the Reason God Made Oklahoma." There was an immediate attraction between the two, which was evident to everyone who witnessed them onstage. Their electrifying performance ended as the six-foot-five Shelton, with a big grin on his face, folded his arms around the five-foot-four Lambert in a long embrace.

Chemistry

Lambert recalls that the whole experience made her very nervous. She wondered at first if it was simply being on stage with another star, especially considering that he was a bigger star than she was at the time. Later she thought that perhaps their chemistry together was the reason behind her nervousness. Lambert recalls, "It was like my first duet with some other country star. And I didn't know if it was just initial butterflies because of that or, I don't know what it was. It was just this draw to each other."[57]

For his part, Shelton comments that he had never had that kind of instant-attraction experience with anybody. The intensity of the moment confused him as well. He says, "I was a married guy, you know? Standing up there and singing with somebody and going, 'Man, this shouldn't be happening.' Looking back on that, I was falling in love with her, right there on stage."[58]

Nothing happened at first, however. Despite their obvious mutual attraction, the romance took time to blossom. After all, Shelton was still married, and Lambert was in a long-term relationship.

For the time being they remained only friends, occasionally writing songs together but avoiding the possibility of romance. Lambert says, "I knew he was married. I had seen their wedding picture in *Country Weekly*. I knew better, like, this is off limits.

Miranda Lambert poses for a portrait at her Texas home in 2005, the year she met Blake Shelton.

My parents are private investigators, for God's sake. I've seen this my whole life—affairs. Of all people to know better, I know better than this."[59]

Meanwhile, Shelton's marriage was fraying, and he and his first wife, Kaynette, parted ways in 2006. After the divorce, the singer left Nashville and moved back to Oklahoma, settling on a farm near the small town of Tishomingo. During this period he also spent significant periods of time in Nashville, where he lived in a rented house.

In December 2005 Shelton branched out a little into another medium besides music, when he made his first appearance on film. Several of his songs were featured in a TV movie, *The Christmas Blessing*, which starred Neil Patrick Harris, Rebecca Gayheart, Angus T. Jones, and Rob Lowe. The singer also had a small role at the end of the movie, playing himself at a benefit concert. His focus remained firmly on music, however, and he was steadily becoming more prominent.

Chapter 4

Widespread Fame

By 2006 the singer was rarely spending time in Oklahoma, because his career kept him on the run. His accomplishments, in addition to a busy concert schedule, included a steady string of recordings, including his 2007 album, *Pure BS*.

In what was becoming a routine pattern for his recordings, the album went gold but the singles taken from it did not do as well as hoped for. The first of these singles, "Don't Make Me," peaked only at number twelve on the country charts, and the second, the clever and funny "The More I Drink," reached only a disappointing number nineteen.

Pure BS marked the first time that a Shelton album was not produced entirely by Bobby Braddock. Instead, the team included two other producers, Brent Rowan and Paul Worley. Shelton co-wrote three of the album's songs: "This Can't Be Good," "I Have Been Lonely," and "The Last Country Song." "The Last Country Song" was one of the album's highlights, enlivened by guest appearances from two singers from older generations: John Anderson and the legendary George Jones.

In 2008, *Pure BS* was reissued with three bonus tracks. Shelton wrote two of them, and the third was a cover of pop-jazz singer Michael Bublé's "Home." Shelton was introduced to "Home" by Lambert, who by now was dating Shelton. She secretly loaded it on his iPod and later sang backup on the record. The song became Shelton's fourth number-one hit.

Blake Shelton is photographed backstage during the 2007 CMT Music Awards. Friends say that Shelton has remained unpretentious despite his fame.

As Shelton's popularity soared during this period, some people assumed he would take on the trappings of a privileged celebrity, as so many performers do. He remained easygoing and unpretentious, however, especially around friends and family. His father once commented, "Blake is just Blake. When he's around us, he's as common as anybody can be. We lose track, really, of just how big he's become."[60]

Startin' Fires

Shelton's next album, *Startin' Fires*, was released in late 2008. It was the singer's first collaboration with a new producer: Scott Hendricks, a fellow Oklahoman. The two discovered that they worked well as a team. Hendricks says that although they have fun in the studio, Shelton is also very serious about the task at hand. The producer notes, "We laugh a lot. [But] he's extremely prepared, which for a producer is a dream. He knows the song[s] better than I do."[61]

Startin' Fires included a number of songs that directly reflected Shelton's personal life. For one thing, he co-wrote "Here I Am," a sweetly romantic song that was undoubtedly written with Lambert in mind. Another highlight was "Bare Skin Rug," a slightly risqué song that the two wrote and sang together. Even the songs that he did not write were chosen because he felt a close personal connection them. In particular, he was proud of the compositions that celebrated rural life, such as "Home Sweet Home," "Country Strong," and "Green," which had lyrics that closely reflected Shelton's life. He told a reporter for his hometown newspaper, the *Ada News*:

> That's what I do. I sit with my guitar, plant corn, and watch the deer and hawks. When I left the house this morning, there was camouflage [clothing for hunting] hanging on the clothesline—as redneck as it gets. . . . I can sing ["Green"] with a big smile on my face, confident that people are getting a hundred percent who I am as a person.[62]

Awards and Honors

Every year in Shelton's life brought new events, but 2010 was especially momentous. For one thing, he released three recordings: a greatest-hits album, *Loaded*, and two extended-play CDs with only six tracks each, *Hillbilly Bone* and *All About Tonight*. The former was notable for its title song, a duet with Shelton's fellow singer and close friend, Trace Adkins.

One of Shelton's aims in releasing these "six-packs" (which are shorter but cheaper than full-length albums) was to give fans new material faster and more economically. He commented, "You hear a song on the radio these days, and you just pull out your phone and buy it off the Internet right then, and you forget about it. We're looking for ways to remind people that we still

Miranda Lambert and Blake Shelton pose with the multiple awards each received at the 2010 Country Music Awards.

make albums, and there's still cool music that you may or may not hear on the radio. So we decided to do a six-song album, and it's really cheap! It's like five dollars and change."[63]

In addition to this innovative sales experiment, 2010 saw Shelton receive two major honors. One was being elected Male Vocalist of the Year at the Forty-Fourth Annual Country Music Awards. The other was the highest prize a country performer can win: membership in the legendary radio program called the Grand Ole Opry.

Invited Via Twitter

The Opry may have been around a long time—it started in 1925, when radio was a revolutionary new form of technology—but Shelton's invitation was thoroughly modern. It occurred when Shelton and Trace Adkins appeared at a concert held to celebrate the reopening of the Opry building after a flood caused serious damage. Adkins told the crowd, "You know Blake is famous for doing the Twitter thing; he's always sending tweets. Well, the Grand Ole Opry sent Blake a tweet tonight."[64]

When Adkins handed Shelton an iPhone, a tweet to @blake shelton appeared on both the phone and a background screen that the audience could see. It read, "You're invited to join the Grand Ole Opry! See you on 10/23/10."[65]

Shelton was clearly moved—he had just received perhaps the highest honor a country music performer can get, acknowledging that he had become a genuine star. It took a moment for

Trace Adkins sent this Tweet to Blake Shelton with a surprise invitation to become a member of the Grand Ole Opry.

Grand Ole Opry
@opry

@blakeshelton, you're invited to join the Grand Ole Opry! See you on 10/23/10.

him to collect himself. He leaned on a piano, gave his friend a hug, and told the crowd, "I don't know what I did in the last year or so to turn Nashville's head a little bit, but whatever I did, man, I'm lovin' this. This moment right here is hands-down the highlight of my career. Thank you all so much. Thank you Grand Ole Opry."[66]

The Engagement

As his fans know, 2010 was a momentous year for Shelton on the personal front as well as the professional. Soon after his split with his first wife, he and Miranda Lambert had begun dating. They soon were a solid couple, and in 2010 he introduced the idea of marriage in a very old-fashioned way—he asked her father for permission. Lambert recalls, "He called my dad and got his blessing first. That was so southern and old-school and per-

Blake Shelton and Miranda Lambert celebrated their engagement with a party at Front Porch Farms in Charlotte, Tennessee.

fect."[67] Permission was granted, and Shelton popped the question during a fishing trip. To no one's surprise, Lambert said yes.

All along, the couple had been living separately, an arrangement they continued to maintain after becoming engaged. Shelton's primary home remained his farm in Tishomingo, and after the engagement became official, Lambert (who had been living in Texas) bought a 700-acre (283ha) farm some six miles (9.7km) away from his place. Lambert has since commented that her decision to move was a big step forward in her commitment to Shelton. She recalls, "I fell in love with [the place], but I wasn't sure. I told Blake, 'If I buy this farm and move away from everything I know, are you going to screw up?' He said, 'Buy the farm.' So I did."[68]

The Wedding

At the wedding, on May 14, 2011, the bride wore her mother's white wedding gown and cowboy boots. The groom wore a designer jacket and vest over a pair of Wrangler jeans—new ones. They exchanged vows under an archway made of antlers at the Don Strange Ranch, a historic location near San Antonio, Texas, that hosts large-scale events.

More than five hundred guests attended, including such celebrities as Reba McEntire, Cee Lo Green, Martina McBride, Katherine Heigl, Kelly Clarkson, Dierks Bentley, Charles Kelley, and the Bellamy Brothers. Not surprisingly, the party afterwards featured plenty of music. A highlight was Shelton's performance of a new song he had written, "Let's Grow Old Together." The reception provided the guests plenty to eat and drink. Singer Joe Nichols comments, "It was a beautiful ceremony, and I've never seen so much ribbon, venison and bourbon in the same room."[69] As for the honeymoon, the couple went fishing.

Less than two weeks later, Shelton and Lambert sang in public for the first time as husband and wife. The occasion was a ceremony inducting Shelton's mentor and friend, Bobby Braddock, into the Country Music Hall of Fame. They performed one of his most famous songs, "Golden Ring," and Braddock commented that the gesture moved him deeply. He commented,

Miranda Lambert shows off her wedding ring during a performance with husband Blake Shelton in May 2011.

"I was just blown away that they would come. . . . It really, really touched me."[70]

In 2011 Shelton also released a new album, *Red River Blue*. Unsurprisingly, it was yet another hit. Fans downloaded its first single, "Honey Bee," from the Internet about 138,000 times within the first week of its release. The single was certified gold after only seven weeks—the fastest gold certification by a male country singer in history. "Honey Bee" became Shelton's ninth number-one single, and the album produced two more number-one hits, including the title song, a duet with Lambert. Furthermore, the album itself debuted at number one.

Many of the songs on *Red River Blue* reflected a shift away from the singer's notorious bad-boy image. Several reviewers noted that, as he settled into married life, Shelton seemed to be mellowing. *Entertainment Weekly* critic Melissa Maerz commented:

> He's lost some rascal magnetism, but he's winning sweetness points, harmonizing with the missus on the title track, offering to make dip for her "tater chips," and insisting, "Let other fools go paint the town / We'll just hold this sofa down." Spoken like a true domestic outlaw. Shelton's a natural-born husband—part lover, part joker—and producer Scott Hendricks plays up his traditional side well on the hard-twanging anthems "Good Ole Boys" and "Hey."[71]

"The House That Built Me"

That same year, 2011, Lambert's busy career paid off when she received a major award of her own. It was for "The House That Built Me," a song she had released the year before on her album *Revolution*.

The song's poignant lyrics are told from the point of view of a woman standing in front of her childhood house. She asks the current owner if she can come in for a nostalgic look around. She promises to take away only her bittersweet memories of the place, such as the spot where her dog was buried and the bedroom where she did her homework and practiced the guitar.

The first time Lambert heard "The House That Built Me," she burst into tears. The singer did not write the song, but it seemed to speak directly to her. She has commented many times that it is a perfect description of much of her life growing up.

Scott Hendricks, Shelton's producer, had originally proposed that Blake record the song, feeling that it could be a huge hit. Hendricks told Shelton, "It could change your career. It'll be Song of the Year, I promise you."[72] But the composition meant so much to Lambert that Shelton insisted that she have it, instead.

Blake Shelton kisses Miranda Lambert at a lavish party celebrating her first number-one record in February 2010.

Another Huge Hit

As Hendricks predicted, "The House That Built Me" was a huge hit. It shot up the charts, stayed at number one for three weeks (making it Lambert's first number-one hit), and quickly went platinum. It went on to win Song of the Year at the annual Country Music Association Awards and again at the Academy of Country Music Awards.

Lambert's album *Revolution* also won several awards—notably Album of the Year from both the Academy of Country Music and the Country Music Association. As if that wasn't enough, Lam-

No Apologies

In this passage, Shelton reflects on his own personality, the mistakes he's made over the years, how his lifestyle resembles that of many of his fans, and how he remains unapologetic about his actions:

> [Audiences have been] trained all these years that country music acts they're listening to are going to go on about how life is so great—that they live this role-model lifestyle. I don't know how that happened over the years. Man, I'm not that guy. I'm not going to suggest that anybody look up to me as their hero and inspiration. I've made some bad mistakes along the way.
>
> I'm not trying to be a politician and preach to people. I'm not that guy. I'm a guy that loves listening to Hank Williams, Jr. albums and get drunk out by the campfire and feel like crap the next day. I'm one of those guys—probably like the guys that are buying my records. I'm just like them.
>
> I think me being open about that is probably why there's a deeper connection with my audience. And hopefully I'm getting a deeper connection with those that weren't or aren't my fans because the respect that I'm not full of bull----. . . .
>
> I'm pretty open to anybody's lifestyle and what they're into. I think I'm more open than what most people would ever imagine. I just take offense to when somebody attacks my lifestyle.

Source: Dave Dawson. "Interview with Blake Shelton." *Dave's Diary*, February 12, 2011. www.nucountry.com.au/articles/diary/february2011/210211_blakeshelton_feature.htm.

bert earned a Grammy Award in 2011 for Best Female Country Vocal Performance. (Her husband was also a nominee that year for "Hillbilly Bone," his duet with Trace Adkins.)

Together, Lambert and Shelton wrote and recorded another song during this period that had a powerful personal meaning.

For years, Shelton had resisted writing about his late brother, Richie, but now Lambert encouraged him to try it. The result was "Over You," which Lambert included on her album *Four the Record* in 2012.

She was the one who recorded it, not her husband, because Shelton thought he could not handle the powerful emotions that singing it onstage, night after night, would bring up. Shelton believes that that this is an important part of his performance style. He comments, "I feel a responsibility when I sing . . . to deliver it in a way that's believable and emotional to people. You kind of have to step out of the song a little bit and sing it, I guess. I don't know how to explain it. It is just something that I do and you have to hold your emotions in, to the point where you don't cry."[73]

Dick Shelton Passes Away

There were many high points during this period of Shelton's life, but there were also some low points. The most wrenching of these concerned Shelton's father. Dick Shelton's health had been declining for years, but his condition worsened throughout 2011. He died of pneumonia in January 2012 at the age of seventy-one.

Soon after his father's death, Shelton made a surprising and touching discovery while going through some of his own things. It was the letter of advice that Dick had written to him years earlier, when the aspiring singer had just arrived in Nashville. The singer relates:

> It was [in] one of those cans you get at Christmas with four different types of popcorn. And if I did one thing right when I was 17, it was saving that letter inside that can. [There was a lot] about how to treat people, how to get respect, how to look people in the eye, and how to shake their hand—basically, how to be a man in the world. It was like I was having a conversation with him I never had.[74]

All in all, 2010 and 2011 were tumultuous years for Shelton and Lambert, with both joy and sorrow. The period included

Catching an Intruder

Of course, Shelton's life has in some ways become typical of the celebrity life. But as often as possible he is just like any "ordinary" person, doing things anyone would do—such as watching TV, spending time with family, tending to his property, or pursuing hobbies.

And sometimes, everyday life throws him a curveball. One example of this came in the summer of 2007, when he helped a family member catch a criminal. The singer was staying with his mother and stepfather at their house in Ada when they received a call from Blake's uncle, Dempsey Byrd, that a drunken man had invaded his house. Shelton's mother tells the story:

> Blake was over at the house, and Dempsey called and said there was a strange man in his house. He said he woke up and there was a big man in his house, so Blake and I just jumped in the truck and went over there. Blake knocked on the door and the man sort of stumbled over and opened it, and Blake said, "Hey, you're in my house, man."

The singer told the man to step out on the porch while his mother went inside. Blake kept the intruder on the porch while his mother called the police, and authorities later charged the man with first-degree burglary and public intoxication.

His mother, joking that she was disappointed the police didn't ask her son for his autograph, adds:

> I'm not even sure they [police] recognized him, to be honest. Blake just happened to be home in Tishomingo and had come over to the house. I don't think he would have guessed he'd end up helping arrest a man and then end up in the police reports.

Source: "Blake Shelton Helps Thwart Intruder." *Christian Views on Country Music*, July 14, 2007. http://country-christian.blogspot.com/2007/07/blake-shelton-helps-thwart-intruder.html.

hit records, growing fame, a marriage, multiple honors, and a father's death. Lambert comments, "It was like everything you could throw at us like cannonballs. You picture newlywed bliss and really it [is us] on the road and us in the hospital a lot of the time. It was just a lot to deal with. It seemed that when that one-year anniversary hit, we could almost go 'Phew, okay, now we're ready.'"[75]

There also was one thing more that happened during this period: that television show called *The Voice*.

On TV

When the show's executives approached Shelton about becoming a judge, the singer resisted at first. He was still indifferent about reality shows, and he already had a busy schedule. But he changed his mind when he heard that another top singer, pop diva Christina Aguilera, had signed on. As he later told a reporter, "I was, like, . . . who am I to be the holdout?' I'm the country guy nobody's ever heard of."[76] Plus, it just sounded like fun. So Shelton signed up to be a judge in the show's first season in the spring of 2011.

The Voice, as its millions of fans know, has a concept similar to other reality vocal competitions, such as *America's Got Talent* and *American Idol*. Its rules have evolved over the seasons, but, simply put, the producers begin by auditioning and choosing singers from around the country (some of them are amateurs, some professional or semiprofessional). Then the contestants are divided into teams that perform, alone and in combinations, before a panel of judges. The number of singers in each group has varied from eight to sixteen, depending on the season.

The judges offer criticism, both positive and negative, after each performance, and they vote to eliminate singers or keep them in competition. During the initial auditions, judges turn their backs to the performers, facing the audience, so that they cannot see who is on stage. A positive response to a performer is made when a judge presses a button. That judge then turns to face the stage and see which contestant he or she has chosen.

A contestant who is chosen joins the team of the judge who responded positively. (If more than one judge presses the button, the singer gets to pick which one to work with.) These teams then continue to rehearse and perform. Judges, meanwhile, act as mentors and coaches for their respective teams. In addition to these main coaches, teams get periodic help from guest singers who are not regulars on the show. In the case of contestants on Team Blake, these outside mentors have included fellow Oklahoman Reba McEntire.

The cast members of the first season of **The Voice** *include (from left to right) host Carson Daly, Cee Lo Green, Adam Levine, Christina Aguilera, and Blake Shelton.*

Members of the viewing audience choose the show's winners from among the finalists. Contestants with the lowest scores are eliminated. The audience can vote for their favorites via phone messages, texts, emails, Twitter, and online purchases of the performers' recordings.

Following the competition throughout a season is exciting, tension-filled, and fun, as the number of contestants is gradually whittled down. The competition is intense and spirited. And when a winner is finally chosen at the end of the season, he or she gets a serious cash reward, a record deal with a major label, and, of course, widespread exposure to the public.

A Smash

The Voice was a smash hit from the beginning. Much of its appeal lies with the individual contestants, of course, but audiences also love seeing the characteristics and personal styles of the judges. There were three other judges during the show's first seasons besides Shelton, each a prominent singer in a different genre: rocker Adam Levine, pop singer Christina Aguilera, and hip-hop singer Cee Lo Green. In the years since the show's debut, the membership of the panel has periodically changed to include such stars as Shakira, Usher, Pharrell Williams, and Gwen Stefani. Shelton and Levine are the only original judges still on the show, and Carson Daly has been the show's host throughout.

Over the seasons, the public personas of these judges have developed and changed. In particular, Shelton has created a significant on-air relationship with Levine; their unlikely pairing lends the program a funny, bantering atmosphere. Writer Josh Eels comments:

They're a great odd couple: the tattooed rock star with his collection of Harleys and the drawling country singer with his beat-up Chevy pickup. . . . "The guy is just pure positive energy," says Adam Levine. "He has this kind of punk-rock mentality, where he's not afraid to speak his mind, not

An Unusual Gift

Celebrities often receive gifts from their fans. Shelton once got a rather unusual and—at least at first—scary present: an iguana. He recalls:

> We were playing a fair, and a few people were handing me stuffed animals and flowers, but one person handed me a paper sack. So I took all the stuff back to the bus. I put the sack in my lap and opened it, and a live iguana jumped out of the sack and onto my shirt. I screamed like a little girl! I think it took a year off my life—it scared the crap out of me.

Source: Billy Dukes. "10 Things You Didn't Know About Blake Shelton." Taste of Country, http://tasteofcountry.com/blake-shelton-things.

afraid to say the wrong thing. It's a huge part of his success: What you get is different than what you're expecting."[77]

From the Heartland

In the singer's opinion, his popularity with *The Voice* audiences is due to his being one of the few country singers to regularly appear on national TV, which means that the music's core audience is underrepresented. This core audience is frequently characterized as coming from the nation's "heartland"—not from Los Angeles, California, or New York City, New York, where most TV shows are produced. This audience, Shelton says, easily relates to his laid-back, down-home style. He comments, "Sometimes I think they [TV producers] don't know who all of us are in the middle. If there's one thing special about me, it's that I seem familiar. People feel like I live next door."[78]

Unsurprisingly, *The Voice* has had widespread repercussions for Shelton. As his career hits a new plateau, thanks to the show's hit status, the singer has been careful to mention publicly that he is properly grateful. Blake comments, "I've always had just enough success to buy me some more tour dates and another record. I was always this close to going to the next level, and I owe [my greater success] to the show for sure."[79]

The Voice finally launched him, after years of being a solid star in the world of country, into the whole new level of celebrity that he had sought for so long. That momentum has not slowed down. On the contrary—his career has reliably risen to new high points.

Chapter 5

On with the Show

Shelton talks frequently about how much he enjoys appearing on *The Voice*, especially as a mentor to aspiring singers. He told one reporter, "That's fun for me, to see new artists and . . . tell them things that have happened to me. I don't like being preached to, so I try not to do that. But I am open to them about advice, and I think they appreciate it."[80]

He prides himself on treating his team right. In the first season, for example, one contestant reached the finals, but the dress she wanted for the occasion was more than the wardrobe budget allowed—so Shelton paid for it himself. He remarks, "Yeah, I spoil them pretty bad. But . . . man, this business is hard. And I've been real lucky."[81]

Furthermore, he enjoys being around his fellow judges. In preparation for the show's seventh season, marking the beginning of Gwen Stefani's turn in a judge's chair, he commented, "I love her. I've never met her, but clearly I'm a fan. . . . I'm anxious to be around anybody like that, I think. I admire her work ethic and think she'll be good for the show. I feel sorry for her, because she's going to lose—to me—but I'll be nice about it."[82]

Team Blake

Not surprisingly, the show has brought luck to the members of successive Team Blakes. Each season has seen at least one of them place in the top three. In season one, singer-songwriter

Dia Frampton came in second. In season two, rhythm-and-blues singer Jermaine Paul was champion. In season three, pop/country artist Cassadee Pope was the champion, with Scottish rocker Terry McDermott the runner-up. And the fourth season saw two more winners emerge from Team Blake: champion Danielle Bradbery, a country singer from Texas, and the third-place winners, the Oklahoma-bred country duo the Swon Brothers.

Shelton's appearances on *The Voice* have changed the face of country music. The genre has always been an important part of popular music, notably as an outgrowth of the kinds of folk music brought to America by early Scottish and English settlers. As reporter Ben Sisario notes, "Country has long been a mainstay of American music."[83]

For a long time, however, country was a relatively small part of the overall music scene, overshadowed by rock and pop. That has changed dramatically in recent years. According to *Billboard* magazine, country music is now the most popular radio format in the nation for music—more so even than hip-hop. (Among all types of radio stations, it is surpassed only by talk radio.)

Much of the credit for this dramatic rise in popularity can be attributed to Shelton's appearances on *The Voice*. Shelton's role on the program has introduced country music to an immense new audience. One measure of the singer's role in broadening country music's audience is that in 2013 the Academy of Country Music presented the singer with its Gene Weed Special Achievement Award, which recognizes "unprecedented, unique and outstanding individual achievement in country music."[84]

But no one has benefited more from Shelton's appearances on *The Voice* than the singer himself. Previously, he had been a top star among country music fans, but crossover superstardom (that is, the ability to appear on pop sales charts as well as country charts) had eluded him. Now his soaring popularity came with even greater success: The singer's first album after *The Voice* debuted, *Red River Blue*, was also his first to go platinum (that is, to sell one million copies).

There was another measure of his growing fame, as well. In 2012, *People* magazine gave him the nod as "The Sexiest Man Alive." Amused by the award, the singer commented:

Blake's Unfortunate Tattoo

On his left forearm Shelton has a tattoo that the singer designed himself. As an avid hunter and outdoorsman, he thought it would be good for him to have a tattoo that evoked those pastimes. So he chose to get deer tracks inked on his skin.

But there was one problem: the tattoo artist was ignorant about what deer tracks look like. So the singer drew a design as best he could. The result: something that Shelton calls "the crappiest tattoo—not only in country music, but maybe the world."

He adds, "To this moment, people still come up to me and say, 'Man, ladybugs . . . that's cool. What does that mean to you?'" After enough people made comments about it, he finally returned to a tattoo parlor to add a design of barbed wire to make it "more manly."

Source: Alanna Conaway. "Blake Shelton Irked by His Ink." *The Boot,* September 25, 2009. http://theboot.com/blake-shelton-irked-by-his-ink.

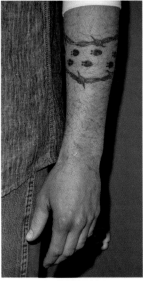

People have misinterpreted the figures depicted in Blake Shelton's tattoo.

I didn't really understand what the deal was. So I said some stupid stuff! Then I found out it was a big deal. . . . So I don't think they know me very well! But my favorite thing about it is that I know my mom, who cuts hair in Ada, Okla., will cut that page out of the magazine and tape it to her mirror and point it out to everybody who comes to the shop.[85]

Committed

Despite such honors and the spike in his popularity, Shelton has publicly stated his concern about the amount of time he spends on the show. The singer knows that his success there could easily lead to more television and film appearances. But he is concerned that this will affect his ability to maintain a high-level career in music—and he has no plans to give up his first love. The singer told a reporter:

> I have a lot to maintain and more to accomplish in the C&W [country and western] music world; it's been very good to me . . . maybe more than I deserve. I probably won't turn down other opportunities if they fall into my lap, but pursue the movie thing . . . nah, can't chance letting my main thing get away from me.[86]

Shelton's commitment to music can be seen in his continuing string of releases. One of these was Shelton's first single in 2013, "Sure Be Cool If You Did." In a novel twist, it became the first song released anywhere, by any artist, in that year. It was available for download from iTunes just a few minutes after midnight on New Year's Eve. "Sure Be Cool If You Did" took only one week to hit the top spot on *Billboard's* Country Digital Tracks chart—a record for Shelton.

Several more singles followed, all taken from the album *Based on a True Story. . . .* The songs were "Boys 'Round Here," "Mine Would Be You," and "Doin' What She Likes." Each song shot to the top, giving Shelton a total of eleven consecutive number-one singles on the country charts. This broke a record previously held by Brad Paisley. Meanwhile, the album itself debuted at number one on the country charts.

In this album Shelton experimented with mixing traditional country with other styles. For example, he added spice to the introduction to "Doin' What She Likes" by running a banjo

Blake Shelton performs in Kansas City, Missouri, in 2013, while promoting his album **Based on a True Story.**

through a device called a wah-wah pedal to distort the sound. Shelton says, "[I] wanted to really push it with sounds and things. . . . I never heard anything like it. It just sounds so cool. And that was important to me, to do things like that."[87]

Cheers and Sunshine

Another 2013 release was a holiday album, *Cheers, It's Christmas.* It featured a number of collaborations with other singers, including a duet with his wife on a lively version of "Jinglebell Rock." Other duets included a remake with Michael Bublé of the latter's "Home."

Shelton even sang a duet with his mother, Dorothy Shackleford: "Time for Me to Come Home," a song that they co-wrote. To accompany the song, Shelton's mother wrote a novel of the same title. The song is about something the singer's mom knows well: having a son who is a big country music star. In the song, the singer is homesick at Christmastime and is trying to get back to his small Oklahoma town in time to open presents.

Not surprisingly, *Cheers, It's Christmas* peaked at number one on Billboard's Top Holiday Albums and number two on its Top Country Albums chart.

The following year, 2014, saw the release of *Bringing Back the Sunshine*, the singer's eleventh studio album. Its overall tone is one of hope triumphing over adversity; the album's first single, "Neon Light," is a witty song about a man seeing the "neon light" at the end of the tunnel after a bad breakup. The album's cover art reflects this theme of optimism after a dark period: It is a stark black-and-white photo of sunbeams shining through clouds above a water tower. (The tower is the one in the singer's hometown of Ada.)

Throughout his career, Shelton has remarked that he is happy and grateful that music has brought him to a good place in life—an attitude that is reflected by his choice of recordings such as "Neon Light." He told a reporter, "I want to be that guy on my albums right now because I don't have that dark cloud I've had before and that we've all had in our lives. If you listen to [one of my later albums], by the end you'll go, 'Man, this guy's pretty happy with his lot in life!' And I am."[88]

The Benefit for Oklahoma

In the spring of 2013, Shelton took on a new role: as the key organizer of a benefit concert. This nationally televised special, "Healing in the Heartland," raised an estimated $6 million to help the victims of a tornado that had recently struck Oklahoma.

The tornado had killed twenty-four people, injured many more, and left hundreds of houses damaged or destroyed. Shelton commented that raising money was simply the right thing to do, telling reporters, "People have given so much to us over the years, and it's times like this when you can give back. You have to. It's not a question of 'Will you?' You have to step up."[89]

One of the show's highlights was the finale, a duet between Shelton and Usher, who was then a fellow judge on *The Voice*.

Acknowledging his friend's fame and talent, Shelton noted, "I'm not that smart, but I'm smart enough to know that if Usher wants to help you, you let him."[90] During the concert, Shelton repeated his admiration for his friend when he grinned and asked the audience, "Man, is there anyone in the world cooler than Usher?"[91]

Usher is not from Oklahoma and has no particular ties to the state. Other performers on the benefit show, however, did have Oklahoma roots. They included Darius Rucker, Carrie Underwood, Rascal Flatts, Reba McEntire, Vince Gill, and—no surprise—Miranda Lambert, who sang "The House That Built Me" and was so overcome that she cried onstage. Shelton ended the show with a spoken tribute to the people affected by the disaster, saying, "You're in our hearts."[92]

At Home

As they have settled into their lives together, the couple has clearly set down permanent roots in Oklahoma. They have gradually expanded their property in the Tishomingo area, which today encompasses a 1,200-acre (486ha) main ranch; a 2,100-acre (850ha) ranch nearby; and the 700-acre (283ha) ranch that Lambert bought when they were dating.

Shelton and Lambert spend as much time as possible there. Shelton compares the experience to recharging a phone. He comments, "It's a small-town atmosphere, and life's a lot slower down here. What I need when I come in off the road or from L.A. to recharge is that type of atmosphere and that state of mind."[93]

In their rare leisure hours together, both Shelton and Lambert still love to hunt and fish. Tending to their pets is also an important part of their lives. This is mostly Lambert's doing, although Shelton did have a pet during the early years of his career—a turkey named Turkey. Until his death, Turkey traveled with the singer on tour. Shelton joked at the time that he was doing it solely for the big bird's benefit:

I feel a responsibility to my pet turkey, Turkey, to expose him to some different things in the world. Up until this

Staying Honest

Shelton stresses that he and his wife have an equal partnership and keep nothing from each other, especially when it comes to the possibility of outside romance. In this excerpt, he reflects on this:

> [I tell Miranda] . . . "Here's my phone. Go through it." That's really the kind of trust we have. There are no secrets. [I'll say,] "Go dig through my drawers or my computer if you feel like you need to." And that's been a really good thing, because I don't want her to ever have any doubts.
>
> I guarantee you, if I saw some guy flirting with my wife, it would p--- me off. Of course, I haven't seen a man brave enough to do that—mostly because I think they'd be afraid of *her* reaction.

Source: Alison Moodie. "I Have Nothing to Hide." *Daily Mail* (UK), May 29 2013. www .dailymail.co.uk/tvshowbiz/article-2332769/Blake-Shelton-says-lets-wife-Miranda -Lambert-dig-phone-blasts-cheating-rumours.html.

point, he's been to Arkansas one time. He has been to Oklahoma, which is where he was born, and now he lives in Tennessee. So, I feel like, without me, he doesn't get to do things, and I feel a responsibility to show him the world.[94]

Shelton later said that dealing with animals—live ones, anyway—is mostly up to his wife. Lambert rides horses and tends to an ever-changing menagerie of dogs, cats, and other creatures. As of 2014 the dog count at her house was six, all of them rescued from shelters or the side of the road. She says that the number is good, telling a reporter, "I'm pretty sure if I got any more I'd be short a husband."[95]

His wife's love of animals is so strong, Shelton claims, that he sometimes doubts his place in her heart. He jokes, "[I]f her dog is in the highway and I'm right there next to it and a semi is coming, I know who she's going to save. It's going to be her dog."[96]

Shelton says he generally likes Lamberts's variety of pets, but he admits to one exception: the felines. He says, "I'm not too big on cats. . . . [Cats are] sneaky, [but] to be fair, if they could send a Tweet, I'm sure they would say something bad about me."[97]

Although the singers spend most of their time in Tishomingo, Oklahoma, it is not their only home. Since they spend significant time in Nashville, Tennessee, the couple also have a place there, and they lease a house in Los Angeles, California, when *The Voice* is in production.

Shelton says he is lukewarm on life in California, however. He refuses to buy a house there and claims he has driven around Los Angeles only a handful of times, preferring to have someone else chauffeur him—mostly between the studio and his house. He told a reporter, "I like California, but I'm dyed-in-the-wool Oklahoma. I see a deer in L.A., and everybody's standing around it taking pictures. Back home, that's the enemy!"[98]

On the other hand, his wife says that she likes life in California—at least in one respect. She loves the weather, especially when compared to Tishomingo's rough winters. She comments, "When we leave Oklahoma, we're leaving 20-degree weather and it's snowing and sleeting, and we get to L.A. and it's sunny and 75, and I'm just, like. . . . 'Oh, thank goodness.'"[99]

Rumors

Shelton and Lambert's marriage and subsequent rise in popularity have made them country music's most prominent couple. Unsurprisingly, they have also become the focus of gossip and rumor. In particular, questionable reports about their marital problems surface constantly. Shelton and Lambert generally ignore these stories and consider them to be nothing but nonsense. She told a reporter:

> Most of it's lies anyways. At first it was a little bit of a pain, but then I finally just realized that it just doesn't matter

anyway. No one pays attention to it. It's just kind of point-less, and I just sort of removed myself from it. I know now that all the stories I read about me or anybody else are

Blake Shelton and Miranda Lambert attend the 2014 Grammy Awards in Los Angeles, California. Despite rumors to the contrary, the couple say that their marriage continues to thrive.

probably not true. So I just brush it off and go about my life.[100]

Still, Shelton and Lambert like to have fun mocking the most outrageous of the rumors. For example, in April 2014 Shelton responded on Twitter to the latest rumor, that they were splitting up because of his drinking and his resistance to having a baby. He tweeted, "Me and @mirandalambert are reading about our separation. . . . I hope I get all the liquor in the divorce!!!" His wife responded by tweeting, "AND the imaginary baby?!"[101]

A Changed Man

Rumors about alcohol and imaginary babies aside, the couple seem to be happy together, and they have clearly changed each other's lives for the better. For his part, Shelton says, "Learning to not be selfish is what has changed in me the most since being married. I'm thinking on behalf of someone else [now]. Just like I hope she's doing with me."[102]

Shelton says that his wife has also toned down his bad-boy carousing. He points out that he is much more stable than during his single days. The singer told a reporter, "I grew tired of going out drinking until 7 A.M. and then waking up at noon and eating pizza. . . . Now if I want to go drinking, I only want to sit at the house with Miranda watching [television]. . . . She really is that rock for me and the center of all of this."[103]

These days, Shelton frequently uses his reputation for drinking as a running joke. He pretends to be slightly drunk as a form of entertainment, but those close to the singer says it is only that—a joke. His mother asserts, "He likes to make people think he's drunk, but I've never seen that boy drunk in my life."[104]

Meanwhile, Lambert says that the positive influence of marriage works both ways. She comments, "Blake is outdoorsy, outspoken and really funny. I used to have no sense of humor. Everything was a big deal. I've gotten so much better about not taking things too seriously—and Blake is the reason why."[105]

Miranda may have mellowed somewhat along with her husband, but she has not lost her reputation as a feisty female.

Always a Tease

Shelton loves to tease his wife. He told a reporter:

I'm always pestering her. I just cannot get enough because she gets irritated so quickly. Maybe I'll tell her one of her dogs is missing, let her believe it for 10 minutes or so. It's terrible! Anything I can think of to get a rise out of her is a sport for me.

But the teasing can also hide a very sweet gesture. For example, the couple once spent a precious week off together at their ranch. Shelton told his wife that he wanted to spend part of it on a road trip around Oklahoma. She was not excited at the prospect but agreed. In fact, he had secretly arranged for them to instead to drive to an airport and board an airplane to Cancun, Mexico, where they stayed at a condo owned by Reba McEntire and her husband.

Source: Kevin O'Donnell. "Blake Shelton: 'I Have Nothing to Hide.'" *People*, June 10, 2013, www.people.com/people/archive/article/0,,20705081,00.html.

Shelton often jokes that he's still a little scared of her. He told one reporter, "I don't [pester her too much]. That's like poking a bear."[106]

Dealing with Celebrity

Shelton and Lambert try hard to maintain as normal a life as possible, but it is always difficult, considering their celebrity status. Their faces are too familiar from constant exposure in the media. Lambert jokes, "I can't even go to Walmart anymore!"[107]

One aspect of Shelton's attempt to maintain a normal life is his effort to keep in touch with many of his childhood friends. One such friend is Jayson "Buck" Gray, who has known the singer since he was ten. As children, they used to go bass fishing at a pond near the Shelton house in Ada.

Blake Shelton fights his way through a crowd and paparazzi as he enters a 2013 Grammys party at the Chateau Marmont, a luxury hotel in Los Angeles, California.

Later in life, after Shelton became famous, Gray asked him to be a groomsman at his wedding. The singer drove overnight from Wisconsin to Oklahoma for the ceremony, arriving just in time. He jumped out of his truck, exhausted and not yet fully dressed for the occasion, and asked the groom, "Hey, man, you got some black socks?"[108]

A Rich Man

Such events indicate that Shelton and his wife remain unpretentious despite their celebrity status. Of course, their success and fame have also made them wealthy. According to *Billboard* magazine, in 2014 Shelton ranked twenty-seventh among the wealthiest music artists, earning more than $10 million in 2013 alone. Estimates of his personal wealth vary widely but are certainly in the tens of millions.

Since the beginning of his career, Shelton has been conservative with this income, saving and investing wisely for the future. He knows that the public can be fickle, and that someday he might not enjoy as much success as he does now. The singer told a financial magazine:

> The only thing that I've figured out is, just keep a good handle on your spending, and knowing that this is only going to last a few years, and you're going to have to treat like these few years are going to have to last you for the rest of my life.
>
> I'm always looking at it like [the latest album] could be my last. . . . I'm not really a big spender. The only thing I've really spent on is land. . . . I've worked too hard to be risky.[109] .

Endorsing Pizza Hut

Recently, a significant portion of Shelton's income has started coming from his association with various companies and the endorsement of products. Endorsing a product can be an extremely lucrative proposition for both a celebrity and the product manufacturer.

As a result, many country stars, such as Carrie Underwood, Taylor Swift, and Faith Hill, have gone that route. Thanks to the rise of country music's popularity, these entertainers are some of the highest-ranked celebrity endorsers. And Shelton is at the top of the pile. *L.A. Times* reporter Randy Lewis comments, "[T]he most effective celebrity musician endorser in the country at the moment is Blake Shelton."[110]

So a number of companies have recruited him to help advertise their products or the charity causes they support. For example, in 2014 the singer acted as a spokesman for JCPenney Cares, a program the company founded to support entertainment programs for military men and women stationed overseas.

But his highest-profile endorsement so far has been with Pizza Hut, a pairing that the singer says is a very comfortable fit. For one thing, he says, he has very fond memories of Pizza Hut—it

Blake Shelton and an actress tape a commercial for Pizza Hut in 2014.

was one of the few options he had as a kid in Ada, when not eating at home. He jokes that Pizza Hut's importance was right up there with Ada's traffic signal and the time when comic actor Don Knotts appeared at a car dealership promotion.

And Shelton has remained a big fan of pizza throughout his life. For example, his tour manager always arranges for concert promoters to include pizza in the food and drink that is supplied backstage for the singer and his crew. And even before the endorsement deal, Shelton specified having Pizza Hut's "Meat-Lover's Pizza" on hand after a show.

He says that he especially likes pizza when it is paired with another of his favorite foods, barbeque. So it was natural that in

2014 he became "the face" of Pizza Hut's new line of barbecue pies. (Not surprisingly, his favorite is a pork-heavy version named after him: "Blake's Smokehouse.")

Furthermore, he says, working with the company has been an enjoyable process. While shooting a TV commercial for the new line of pizzas, he told a reporter, "I'm having a lot of fun working with the Pizza Hut people. They're so much fun to be around. Their headquarters is in Dallas, and that's basically right outside of where I live anyway, so we already have a lot in common. I wish all my workdays were this much fun!"[111]

His wife's business interests have branched out in a similar way. For example, she has started a line of shoes called, naturally, Miranda. She also owns two clothing and antique shops, called the Pink Pistol—one in Tishomingo and one in her hometown of Lindale, Texas. (The name comes from her two favorite words.)

Then there is Ladysmith, a bed and breakfast that Lambert opened in a historic Tishomingo building, which she called "too beautiful a building not to restore."[112] She also has wine, coffee, and clothing companies—not to mention the company devoted to dog accessories. She told a reporter, "I've always said I want to build an empire. I don't think my empire will be in New York City in a high-rise. My empire is more of a backyard circus tent."[113]

Overall, despite his riches and celebrity, Shelton clearly intends to maintain his unpretentious, simple, and stress-free life—as much as possible, anyway. He says that he has a basic set of long-term goals: "Do well enough to spend a lot more time in Tishomingo with Miranda; keep the possums out of my watermelon patch, my deer stand in good repair and the local taxidermist busy with lunker large mouth bass and eight-point bucks; and patronize the local beer joints."[114]

With luck, Shelton will reach those goals and keep on doing what he loves for many years to come.

Introduction: Meet Blake Shelton

1. Quoted in Billy Dukes. "10 Things You Didn't Know About Blake Shelton." *Taste of Country*. www.tasteof country.com/blake-shelton-things.
2. Quoted in Josh Eells. "Blake Shelton, Natural Born Hell-Raiser." *Men's Journal*, August 2013. www.mensjournal .com/magazine/blake-shelton-natural-born-hell-raiser -20130711.

Chapter 1: Blake Grows Up

3. Quoted in Eells. "Blake Shelton, Natural Born Hell-Raiser."
4. Quoted in Keith Eaton. "Blake Shelton: An Oklahoma Original Is Singing His Way Back Home." *Distinctly Oklahoma*, October 4, 2010. www.distinctlyoklahoma.com /cover-story/blake-shelton-an-oklahoma-original-is -singing-his-way-back-home.
5. Quoted in Christina Vinson. "Blake Shelton's Mom Reveals His Boyhood Nickname." *Taste of Country*, July 17, 2013. www.tasteofcountry.com/blake-sheltons-nickname.
6. Quoted in CMT.com. "20 Questions with Blake Shelton." February 5, 2003. www.cmt.com/news/20-questions /1459805/20-questions-with-blake-shelton.jhtml.
7. Quoted in "Blake Shelton: Snapshot." *People*. www.people .com/people/blake_shelton.
8. Quoted in Eaton. "Blake Shelton: An Oklahoma Original Is Singing His Way Back Home."
9. Quoted in Dukes. "10 Things You Didn't Know About Blake Shelton."
10. Quoted in Mabel Jong. "When Investing, Singer Blake Shelton Loves His Land." *Bankrate*, September 11, 2003. www.bankrate.com/brm/news/investing/20030911a1.asp.
11. Quoted in Eaton. "Blake Shelton: An Oklahoma

Original Is Singing His Way Back Home."

12. Quoted in Eells. "Blake Shelton, Natural Born Hell-Raiser."

13. Quoted in Eaton. "Blake Shelton: An Oklahoma Original Is Singing His Way Back Home."

14. Quoted in Eells. "Blake Shelton, Natural Born Hell-Raiser."

15. Quoted in Eells. "Blake Shelton, Natural Born Hell-Raiser."

16. Quoted in Dukes. "10 Things You Didn't Know About Blake Shelton."

17. Quoted in Eells. "Blake Shelton, Natural Born Hell-Raiser."

18. Quoted in CMT.com. "20 Questions with Blake Shelton."

19. Quoted in Eaton. "Blake Shelton: An Oklahoma Original Is Singing His Way Back Home."

20. Quoted in Eaton. "Blake Shelton: An Oklahoma Original Is Singing His Way Back Home."

21. Quoted in *Pollstar*. "Hot Star: Blake Shelton." December 7, 2001. www.pollstar.com/hotstar_article.aspx?ID =75738.

22. Quoted in Dyrinda Tyson. "Team Blake." *Oklahoma Today*, September-October 2011. www.oklahomatoday .com/oklahomatoday/MAGAZINE/Features/SO11_-_Team _Blake_1.html.

23. Quoted in Brandy McDonnell. "Blake Shelton Talks 'Austin,' 'Ol' Red' and Painting Mae Boren Axton's House." *NewsOK*, March 25, 2010. www.newsok.com/blake -shelton-talks-austin-ol-red-and-painting-mae-boren -axtons-house/article/3824798.

Chapter 2: Scuffling

24. Quoted in Tyson. "Team Blake."

25. Quoted in Alison Bonaguro. "Blake Shelton's Lost Letter from His Dad." CMT, July 12, 2013. www.cmt.com/news /cmt-offstage/1710475/offstage-blake-sheltons-lost-letter -from-his-dad.jhtml.

26. Quoted in Jay Orr. "Blake Shelton on His Way with 'Austin,' Help from Industry Veterans." MTV News, August 2, 2001. www.mtv.com/news/1445942/blake-shelton -on-his-way-with-austin-help-from-industry-veterans.

27. Quoted in CMT.com. "20 Questions with Blake Shelton."

28. Quoted in Craig Shelburne. "Blake Shelton Digs Up the Dirt on *Hillbilly Bone*." *CMT Insider News Now*, March 19, 2010. www.cmt.com/news/country-music/1634321/blake -shelton-digs-up-the-dirt-on-hillbilly-bone-part-1-of-2 .jhtml.

29. Quoted in Tyson. "Team Blake."

30. Quoted in *Pollstar*. "Hot Star: Blake Shelton."

31. Quoted in Orr. "Blake Shelton on His Way with 'Austin,' Help from Industry Veterans."

32. Quoted in Shelburne. "Blake Shelton Digs Up the Dirt on *Hillbilly Bone*."

33. Quoted in Marianne Horner. "Story Behind the Song— 'Austin.'" *Country Weekly*, October 23, 2001. www .countryweekly.com/vault/story-behind-song-austin.

34. Quoted in Orr. "Blake Shelton on His Way with 'Austin,' Help from Industry Veterans."

35. Quoted in Horner. "Story Behind the Song—'Austin.'"

36. Quoted in Shelburne. "Blake Shelton Digs Up the Dirt on *Hillbilly Bone*."

37. Quoted in Shelburne. "Blake Shelton Digs Up the Dirt on *Hillbilly Bone*."

38. Quoted in Horner. "Story Behind the Song—'Austin.'"

39. Quoted in *Pollstar*. "Hot Star: Blake Shelton."

40. Quoted in Jong. "When Investing, Singer Blake Shelton Loves His Land."

41. Quoted in *Pollstar*. "Hot Star: Blake Shelton."

42. Quoted in Horner. "Story Behind the Song—'Austin.'"

43. Maria Konicki Dinoia. "Blake Shelton." Allmusic.com. www.allmusic.com/album/blake-shelton-mw0000011139.

44. Scott Homewood. "Blake Shelton." *Country Standard Time*. www.countrystandardtime.com/d/cdreview.asp?xid =208.

45. Quoted in CMT.com. "20 Questions with Blake Shelton."
46. Quoted in Billy Dukes. "10 Things You Didn't Know About Blake Shelton."

Chapter 3: Breakthrough

47. Quoted in Eells. "Blake Shelton, Natural Born Hell-Raiser."
48. Quoted in *Pollstar*. "Hot Star: Blake Shelton."
49. Quoted in *Country Weekly*. "The Story Behind the Song: 'The Baby.'" June 25, 2003. www.countryweekly.com /vault/story-behind-song-baby.
50. Quoted in CMT.com. "20 Questions with Blake Shelton."
51. Quoted in Jong. "When Investing, Singer Blake Shelton Loves His Land."
52. Quoted in Wendy Newcomer. "Chapel of Love." *Country Weekly*, December 13, 2003. www.countryweekly.com /vault/chapel-love.
53. Quoted in Newcomer. "Chapel of Love."
54. Quoted in Cindy Watts. "Blake Shelton Announces Bridgestone Arena Show." *Tennessean*, June 14, 2013. www.blogs.tennessean.com/tunein/2013/06/14/blake -shelton-announces-bridgestone-arena-show.
55. Quoted in CMT.com. "20 Questions with Blake Shelton."
56. Quoted in *Pollstar*. "Hot Star: Blake Shelton."
57. Quoted in Sarah Bull. "'I Knew He Was Married . . . but I Went After Him Anyway!'" *Daily Mail*, September 1, 2011. www.dailymail.co.uk/tvshowbiz/article-2032193 /Miranda-Lambert-knew-Blake-Shelton-married-met .html.
58. Quoted in Melissa Maerz. "Miranda Lambert on Blake Shelton: 'I Knew He Was Married.'" *Entertainment Weekly*, August 30, 2011. www.music-mix.ew.com/2011/08/30 /miranda-lambert-blake-shelton-dateline.
59. Quoted in Maerz. "Miranda Lambert on Blake Shelton: 'I Knew He Was Married.'"

Chapter 4: Widespread Fame

60. Quoted in Tyson. "Team Blake."

61. Quoted in Tyson. "Team Blake."

62. Quoted in *Ada News*. "Blake Shelton: Celebrating Country Life." April 25, 2009. www.theadanews.com /local/x212631009/Blake-Shelton-Celebrating-Country -Life.

63. Quoted in Gayle Thompson. "Blake Shelton Getting Ready for a 'Six Pack' Summer." *The Boot*, June 10, 2010. www.theboot.com/blake-shelton-albums/?trackback =tsmclip.

64. Quoted in *Country Standard Time*. "Opry Returns Home, Shelton Receives Invite." September 29, 2010. www.countrystandardtime.com/news/newsitem.asp?xid =4555.

65. Quoted in *Country Standard Time*. "Opry Returns Home, Shelton Receives Invite."

66. Quoted in *Country Standard Time*. "Opry Returns Home, Shelton Receives Invite."

67. Quoted in Eileen Finan. "Blake Shelton and Miranda Lambert Engaged!" *People*, May 11, 2010. www.people .com/people/article/0,,20368286,00.html.

68. Quoted in Meryl Gordon. "Miranda Lambert: Nashville's Shooting Star." *Ladies Home Journal*, March 2011. www.lhj.com/style/covers/miranda-lambert.

69. Quoted in Michelle Tauber, Danielle Anderson, and Eileen Finan. "Miranda Lambert and Blake Shelton: Our Wedding Album." *People*, July 6, 2011. www.people.com /people/archive/article/0,,20501754,00.html.

70. Quoted in Tyson. "Team Blake."

71. Melissa Maerz. "Red River Blue." *Entertainment Weekly*. July 14, 2011. www.ew.com/ew/article/0,,20355856 _20506394,00.html.

72. Quoted in Tyson. "Team Blake."

73. Quoted in CMT.com. "20 Questions with Blake Shelton."

74. Quoted in Eells. "Blake Shelton, Natural Born Hell-Raiser."

75. Quoted in Wendy Newcomer. "GAC Premieres Back-story: Miranda Lambert January 19." GACTV. www .blog.gactv.com/blog/tag/rick-lambert.
76. Quoted in Eells. "Blake Shelton, Natural Born Hell-Raiser."
77. Quoted in Eells. "Blake Shelton, Natural Born Hell-Raiser."
78. Quoted in Eells. "Blake Shelton, Natural Born Hell-Raiser."
79. Quoted in Eells. "Blake Shelton, Natural Born Hell-Raiser."

Chapter 5: On with the Show

80. Quoted in Tyson. "Team Blake."
81. Quoted in Eells. "Blake Shelton, Natural Born Hell-Raiser."
82. Quoted in Wendy Geller. "Blake Fuels His 'Voice' with New Line of Shelton-Approved Pizzas." *Our Country*, May 8, 2014. www.music.yahoo.com/blogs/our-country /blake-fuels-his--voice--with-new-line-of-shelton-approv ed-pizzas-190308890.html.
83. Ben Sisario. "Good Times Rollin' for Country Music." *Seattle Times*, April 7, 2014.
84. Quoted in Brandy McDonnell. "Blake Shelton to Receive ACM's Gene Weed Special Achievement Award." *NewsOK*, March 25, 2013. www.newsok.com/blake -shelton-to-receive-acms-gene-weed-special-achievement -award/article/3832810.
85. Quoted in Dukes. "10 Things You Didn't Know About Blake Shelton."
86. Quoted in Eaton. "Blake Shelton: An Oklahoma Origi-nal Is Singing His Way Back Home."
87. Quoted in Blakeshelton.com. "Bio." www.blakeshelton .com/bio.
88. Quoted in Blakeshelton.com. "Bio."
89. Quoted in Eric R. Danton. "Blake Shelton, Usher Sing 'Home' at Oklahoma Benefit Concert." *Rolling Stone*, May 30, 2013. www.rollingstone.com/music/videos/Blake

-Shelton-usher-sing-home-at-Oklahoma-benefit-concert
-20130530.

90. Quoted in Eells. "Blake Shelton, Natural Born Hell-
Raiser."

91. Quoted in Ashley Majeski. "Music's Biggest Stars Come
out to Raise Money for Oklahoma Tornado Victims." *USA
Today*, May 29, 2013. www.today.com/entertainment
/musics-biggest-stars-come-out-raise-money-oklahoma
-tornado-victims-1C10124930.

92. Quoted in Majeski. "Music's Biggest Stars Come out to
Raise Money for Oklahoma Tornado Victims."

93. Quoted in Tyson. "Team Blake."

94. Quoted in CMT.com. "20 Questions with Blake
Shelton."

95. Quoted in Lauren Moraski. "Miranda Lambert: I'd Be
'Short a Husband' if I Adopt Another Dog." CBS News,
July 29, 2014. www.cbsnews.com/news/miranda-lambert
-id-be-short-a-husband-if-i-adopt-another-dog.

96. Quoted in Shelburne. "Blake Shelton Digs Up the Dirt
on *Hillbilly Bone*."

97. Quoted in Melody Chiu. "Blake Shelton: I'm Not a Cat
Person." *People*, May 15, 2014. www.people.com/article
/blake-shelton-miranda-lambert-cats.

98. Quoted in Eells. "Blake Shelton, Natural Born Hell-
Raiser."

99. Quoted in Carrie Horton. "Miranda Lambert and Blake
Shelton Buy a House in Nashville." *Taste of Country*, February 28, 2014. www.tasteofcountry.com/miranda-lambert
-blake-shelton-nashville-house.

100. Quoted in Moraski. "Miranda Lambert: I'd Be 'Short a
Husband' if I Adopt Another Dog."

101. Quoted in Brittany Wong. "Blake and Miranda Respond
to Divorce Rumors in the Best Possible Way." *Huffington
Post*, April 2014. www.huffingtonpost.com/2014/04/17
/blake-shelton-miranda-lam_n_5168394.html.

102. Quoted in Kevin O'Donnell. "Blake Shelton: 'I Have
Nothing to Hide.'" *People*, June 10, 2013. www.people
.com/people/archive/article/0,,20705081,00.html.

103. Quoted in "Blake Shelton: How Miranda Lambert Saved Me." June 30, 2011. www.usmagazine.com/celebrity-news/news/blake-shelton-how-miranda-lambert-saved-me-2011306.

104. Quoted in Eells. "Blake Shelton, Natural Born Hell-Raiser."

105. Quoted in Gordon. "Miranda Lambert: Nashville's Shooting Star."

106. Quoted in Eells. "Blake Shelton, Natural Born Hell-Raiser."

107. Quoted in Gordon. "Miranda Lambert: Nashville's Shooting Star."

108. Quoted in Eells. "Blake Shelton, Natural Born Hell-Raiser."

109. Quoted in Joel Stein. "Dixie Schtick: Miranda Lambert's Business Empire." *Bloomberg Businessweek*, July 03, 2014. www.businessweek.com/articles/2014-07-03/country-music-star-miranda-lamberts-business-empire.

110. Randy Lewis. "Would You Buy [Product Name Here] from Blake Shelton? Yes!" *Los Angeles Times*, November 6, 2013. www.articles.latimes.com/2013/nov/06/entertainment/la-et-ms-cma-awards-blake-shelton-celebrity-musician-survey-20131106.

111. Quoted in Geller. "Blake Fuels His 'Voice' with New Line of Shelton-Approved Pizzas."

112. Quoted in Vinson. "Blake Shelton's Mom Reveals His Boyhood Nickname."

113. Quoted in Stein. "Dixie Schtick."

114. Quoted in Eaton. "Blake Shelton: An Oklahoma Original Is Singing His Way Back Home."

1976
Blake Tollison Shelton is born in Ada, Oklahoma, on June 18.

1993
At age seventeen, Shelton moves to Nashville to pursue a career in music.

1998
Shelton signs a recording contract with Giant Records.

2001
Shelton's self-titled debut record is released; both it and its first single, "Austin," become hits.

Shelton is nominated for the Academy of Country Music's "Top New Male Vocalist" award, the first of many award nominations and wins.

2003
Shelton marries his first wife, Kaynette Gern.

2005
Shelton meets singer Miranda Lambert.

2006
Shelton and his first wife divorce.

2010
Shelton is awarded country music's highest honor, membership in the Grand Ole Opry.

Shelton and Lambert become engaged.

2011
Shelton and Lambert are married; Shelton becomes a judge for the first season of *The Voice*.

2012

Blake's father, Dick Shelton, passes away.

2013

Shelton earns a record-breaking, eleventh consecutive number-one hit on the country sales charts, for a total of seventeen number-one records.

2014

Shelton releases *Bringing Back the Sunshine*, his eleventh recording.

For More Information

Books

Risa Brown, *Blake Shelton*. Hockessin, DE: Mitchell Lane, 2014. A brief biography of the singer, part of the Blue Banner Biography series.

Lisa Lee, *This Is Country: A Backstage Pass to the Academy of Country Music Awards*. San Rafael, CA: Insight, 2014. This well-illustrated look at one of the most prestigious organizations in country music contains contributions from many stars, including Blake Shelton.

Sarah Lucas, *290 Success Facts: Blake Shelton—Everything You Need to Know*. Emereo, 2014. This book delivers what the title says: nearly 300 facts about the singer.

Articles and Internet Sources

Dave Dawson, "Interview with Blake Shelton." *Dave's Diary*, February 12, 2011, www.nucountry.com.au/articles/diary /february2011/210211_blakeshelton_feature.htm. This articles features a long interview with the singer.

Lori Berger, "Basic Blake." *Redbook*, February 2012, www.red bookmag.com/fun-contests/celebrity/blake-shelton. This magazine article provides an in-depth profile of and interview with Shelton.

Josh Eells, "Blake Shelton, Natural Born Hell-Raiser. *Men's Journal*, August 2013, www.mensjournal.com/magazine /blake-shelton-natural-born-hell-raiser-20130711. This magazine article is an extensive profile of Shelton.

"Biography: Blake Shelton." Biography.com, www.biography .com/people/blake-shelton-20833401#synopsis. This entry on an encyclopedic website provides a brief overview of the singer's life and accomplishments.

"About Blake Shelton." Country Music Television, www.cmt .com/artists/blake-shelton/biography. This page on the TV network's website includes a brief biography of Shelton.

Websites

BlakeShelton.com (www.blakeshelton.com). The singer's official website, includes news, information about tours and recordings, and more.

@blakeshelton (https://twitter.com/blakeshelton). This social media site is an effective way to become a follower of the singer, who is a huge presence on Twitter.

Blake Shelton Fan Club (www.facebook.com/BlakeShelton FanClub). This is the Facebook page for the singer's fan club, the BS'ers.

Index

Picture Credits

About the Author

Adam Woog is the author of many books for adults, young adults, and children. He also writes a monthly column for *The Seattle Times* and teaches at a preschool. Woog lives in Seattle, Washington, with his wife, and they have a grown daughter.